Strong Getting Stronger

Michael Strong

DEDICATION

To All the staff, students and alumni of the Maryland Center for Veterans Education and Training

Special Thanks to:

LaDonna Comera Roberts Strong, the epitome of a strong black woman, for holding it down when I couldn't.

CONTENTS

Michael Strong

ACKNOWLEDGMENTS

My siblings and I often refer to our parents, John Quincy and Louise Grace Strong, as "King and Queen." They raised us with as much love and nurturing as children need. We were poor but always experienced love and good 'ole fashioned parental support in everything we did.

Many say the system's designed for black children to fail and we've been dealt a bad hand. My parents never fed into that notion but instead taught us to study hard, love unconditionally, respect others and be our best. I made some pretty bad choices along the way, but not because of how I was raised. I humbly and reverently acknowledge my parents for everything they did for me and thank them for continuing to watch over me from above.

I lovingly recognize my daughter, Sade, who never gave up on me. Although it'd been at least twelve years since I'd talked to her or her brother, I opened my email one day to find a message from her and cried all day because I never thought she'd forgive me for being an absent dad. I'm so proud of Sade, our intimate relationship and my precious grandson, Amari. Nowadays Sade and I communicate often and on some days are each other's support systems.

I gratefully acknowledge my siblings: Nora, Bobbi Jean, Gloria, Calvin, Freddie, Sarah, Jerome, Margaret, Hazel, Cynthia, CC, Willie, Mona Lisa, Shawn and Libbie. I love you and thank you for never losing faith in me.

I wholeheartedly recognize people at MCVET, especially Col. Charles Williams for keeping MCVET's vision alive; Dr. Jack Pierce for believing in me; Ms. Vaughn and Ms. Cannon, the most talented case managers in the world; and Dr. Finkelstein, the best therapist anyone could have. Thank you, Dr. Finkelstein, for listening to me when no one else would. I also recognize the fellowship and everyone in my sponsorship family because I could not have done this without you.

Finally, I lovingly acknowledge my son, Michael DeMarkco Strong. DeMarkco may not be able to read or understand this book's contents, but he is my inspiration. I still remember our last trip to a Charlotte amusement park and the way DeMarkco – though partially deaf and autistic – enjoyed the park's sights, sounds and smells more than I or his sister. In DeMarkco I see a shining example of living through the heart. He doesn't understand most things, but the love and innocence he possesses are exhilarating. Because of DeMarkco I now realize it's possible to reach a comfort level with unconditional love, acceptance of others and my own life and circumstances.

"Our scars remind us of where we've been; they don't have to dictate where we're going." -- A profound quote from "Criminal Minds"

Foreword

Unite For Life! was the name of the Piedmont Area Convention of Narcotics Anonymous I attended in August 2006. The convention was full of life, sharing and people meeting people. I had no idea during this trip to Greensboro, N.C.; I'd meet a man named Michael Strong.

Our initial history is pretty basic. We exchanged phone numbers and promised to keep in touch. Then in November 2007 – during one of our many conversations – Michael asked me to sponsor him and guide him through the Twelve Steps. His request and my acceptance resulted in a friendship filled with deep meaning and mutual respect.

I didn't know how we'd connect, but Michael's dedication to step work helped solidify an intimate relationship. Our bond was based on trust that allowed us to delve deeply into Michael's emotions. Working through the Twelve Steps exposed a level of integrity that basically guided Michael's life. The most valuable thing I learned was, instinctively, Michael always leans toward the truth.

During our many conversations I've learned about Michael's childhood, family, children, extensive travels, relationships and reason for being in the world – all of which remind me of his spiritual growth. Although Michael believed in and embraced the concept of God when we met, he needed to resolve unanswered questions to strengthen his faith. Like many of us, Michael needed to make peace with past situations and circumstances. Michael has done a yeoman's job of forgiving himself and others for past transgressions and of becoming a better person; however, he'll be the first to acknowledge he's still a work in progress. Knowing intimately how addicts recover, I can confidently make three statements about Michael: His faith is intact; He genuinely cares for others; He is a contributor. As our friendship has grown, I've realized Michael can do anything he wants. The potential always existed; He simply needed to channel it.

I wasn't surprised when Michael decided to write an autobiography. His gripping, brutally honest book is evidence he's living up to his potential; likewise, it proves he's serious about his recovery. I trust you'll find "Strong Getting Stronger" as engaging as I did. I pray "Strong Getting Stronger" blesses you in some way. And I know whether you're a recovering addict or someone who has never touched drugs or alcohol, "Strong Getting Stronger" will prompt you to self-reflect and make some changes.

Congratulations, Michael!

Don R.

Chapter 1

The Photograph

He removes the leather wallet from his pants and flicks it open as he's done countless times before. Without looking he gropes the contents for a few seconds before pulling out a tiny, laminated photograph displaying a man with sunken cheeks and ashen skin.

The photograph is hideous, but that doesn't stop him from slipping it out of his wallet once a week to take a gander.

The man in the photograph isn't smiling because he has nothing to smile about. In fact, he looks as if his life has spun out of control.

Truth is, when the photograph was taken my life was out of control but thank God it's not anymore. So I'll continue my weekly ritual of looking at the photograph because looking at it helps me stay grounded, humble and grateful.

You see, when the photograph was taken my life was a colossal train wreck.

Today, I have a life.

Coffee, water, juice and soda have replaced Remy Martin, Crown Royal, Hennessey and Corona. I used to smoke crack on the regular; now I hesitate to take Nyquil because it contains ten percent alcohol.

I used to sleep with tons of women, party all weekend and drive a Porsche. Today I practice monogamy, overdose on reading, politics and sports and proudly drive a non-descript vehicle.

Back in the day I was arrogant and impatient and had little tolerance for people I deemed intellectually inferior. Thanks to the Twelve Step program I now practice humility, acceptance and realize everyone's opinion deserves to be heard.

My life is good now because with God's help I've emerged from an existence of drugs, alcohol and pain. It's not perfect, and I don't kid myself about that. Every day is still a struggle, not necessarily to avoid reverting to dope, booze and women but instead the bad habits that led to them in the first place.

Recovering addicts like me who keep it real know addiction comes in many forms. For example, something always made me yearn to be the life of the party, so whether I could afford it I'd buy a round of drinks for bar strangers just to appear cool and be liked.

I'm not bad looking and had no time for women who wouldn't sleep with me on the first date. Fortunately despite my sexual escapades I have only two children by my ex-wife.

My life used to be one big routine: go to work, get high after work and go back to work so on payday I'd have money with which to get high. That was it. Sure there were some women thrown in here and there for good measure – even some serious, long-term relationships – but my primary objective was getting high plain and simple.

These days I busy myself with work, attending Twelve Step meetings, church and working out. I'm a regular at Twelve Step meetings because I need to be. The program is a Godsend and I shudder to think where I'd be without it. Some addicts don't attend many meetings, but as long as I'm breathing I'll frequent them. I don't go only when I'm at home in Baltimore; I also go on vacation. When I lived in North Carolina I often ran meetings at my Greensboro home group, and I'm frequently asked to speak. I accept speaking requests because there have been plenty of times when hearing someone else's story helped me. I say yes because my words just might keep someone from using. I say yes because speaking publicly keeps me grounded, is cathartic and because I strongly believe to whom much is given much is required.

I can't speak for other recovering addicts, but I'm not ashamed of what I am. The past is the past. It is what it is.

Now don't get it twisted. I don't just walk up to virtual strangers and tell them I spent two decades getting high, but I also don't try to hide it. When I start seeing a woman I disclose I'm a recovering addict before emotions get too deep on either side. Blindsiding someone with that kind of news isn't fair, nor does it make sense to wait until I've fallen for someone to tell her because chances are she won't be able to handle it.

I once told a former girlfriend less than forty-eight hours after we met, sooner than I'd planned but when I deemed it necessary. She stopped by one Sunday while a female friend and I were on the patio kicking it. There was nothing romantic between me and my friend, who I'd met through the Twelve Step program, but my new woman didn't know that. I could tell by the look in her eyes – not to mention the way she hurriedly went inside after muttering hello – she wasn't too happy to see me with another woman.

After my friend left I told my woman how we'd met. When I said the words Narcotics Anonymous her eyes widened a bit, but she didn't freak out or bolt.

Though I was interested in her from the time we met, if she'd done an Elvis and left the building I would have been okay.

Listen, I spent twenty years wasting my life. My marriage ended in large part because of my addiction. I have a grown son with whom I've never had the typical father-son relationship and a grown daughter who used to vacillate between loving me and harboring ill feelings over my former lifestyle. I lost a really good-paying job because I got caught stealing while in active addiction. I have to live everyday knowing my dear, sweet mother died not knowing whether I was okay. I've watched a brother and a sister die from complications stemming from drug abuse. I used to go one or two years at a time without communicating with my siblings because when you're on drugs those who matter most really don't matter at all. And very shortly after I got close to my dad he died.

So needless to say I sure as hell can handle a woman's rejection. Likewise, I can easily tell people I'm a recovering addict. So I keep the photograph in my wallet as a stark reminder of my former life and in case I momentarily let down my guard and forget just how far I've come. I keep it so when I see a brother on the street and know he's struggling with drugs I can whip it out and show him before shocking the shit out of him by revealing I'm the horrid looking cat in it. Of course my motive is for him to realize if I can overcome years of drug abuse so can he. Who's to say whether that approach has ever worked? What I do know is if a picture is truly worth a thousand words, the photograph I keep on me at all times is worth a million – easily.

By the way, I am Michael Lee Strong.

Chapter 2

My Parents

When I chose to write this book I had to decide just how forthright to be and whether to disclose only part of my story. Suffice it to say I've decided to go for it.

My childhood was interesting to say the least. For starters, I'm the youngest of six boys and have ten sisters. That's right. There are sixteen children in my family! My mother had nine children and my dad had three when they married and had me and my three younger sisters. That alone is enough to make for an interesting childhood – but there's more.

I grew up on a small farm in Bennettsville, S.C. We had chickens, pigs, ponies and a cow. I vividly remember cutting down trees in the woods, bringing them back to the woodpile and chopping or sawing them into blocks for our stove. My siblings and I learned what hard work meant early on. And don't think I'm referring to only the boys because my sisters had to work hard, too.

Think back to your childhood and the good 'ole days when you played Red Rover, Hide-and-Seek or Kickball in the yard; dashed excitedly toward the melodious, enticing sounds of the ice cream truck as it crept slowly down your street; or enjoyed sleepovers with your friends. And who can forget those great Saturday morning cartoons? I can because we rarely got to watch them. Our parents, particularly our dad, didn't play that. We had to get up unconscionably early on Saturdays and work. While other kids slept late before enjoying hours in front of the tube watching "Speed Racer," "Archie & Friends," "The Jackson 5," "Spiderman" and other cartoons, we were out in the field tending to business. Inclement weather wasn't our friend either because when it was extremely hot or cold or raining outside, we had to work our butts off inside. Dusting. Mopping. Vacuuming. We even had to flip the mattresses and beat them. At the time we probably thought our parents were mean – or at least crazy. But our parents loved us enough to teach us to work hard. They loved us enough not to let us sit idly in front of the TV all day. And let's face it. They didn't have sixteen kids for nothing. In other words mom got help with the housework and dad got help with the yard work so he could make money outside the home. Of course we got to play with neighborhood kids from time to time, and we occasionally got to watch cartoons. My brothers, sisters and I didn't get everything we wanted, but we got everything we needed and there's no question we were loved.

I'd be remiss if I didn't discuss my parents, John Quincy and Louise Grace Strong, so allow me to introduce them.

God has brought me through countless times, especially during the two decades I spent getting high. Eleven years ago I finally realized my choices were to check into a rehabilitation center or end up dead. Thankfully I chose rehab. I know God kept me alive – and relatively safe – when I was strung out, but I also know my parents prayed for me, never gave up on me and trusted Him to help me find my way home.

John Strong was aptly named. When he met my mom she had nine children, which would have made most men run scared. Dad knew when he proposed to mom he'd have to assume responsibility for her nine children, and he proposed anyway. My father loved my mother's nine kids just as much as he loved his three. And of course their union produced four more. Raising and supporting so many kids couldn't have been easy, but my parents did it. And because my father was the epitome of head of the household my mother didn't mind being submissive to him. My father was a good man. He loved my mother. He took care of her. He was her best friend.

At 6'4", John Strong was an imposing man. He was lean, handsome, tough and a man's man. My dad was a farmer, carpenter, mechanic, nightclub owner and moonshiner – a regular jack-of-all-trades. Despite his numerous and varied jobs, my dad was home every night to constantly shower mom with mad love and respect. When you saw my parents together you saw and felt the love, just like with President Barack Obama and his lovely wife Michelle. My dad wasn't into that macho bull. He was unabashed about his feelings for mom and didn't conceal them.

Dad was a loving husband and a stern and loving father. He stressed education and hard work though he had only a fourth grade education. He told me to study hard, stay away from drugs and treat women with respect. To put it simply, I had one hell of a father.

Michael Strong

Louise Strong is the sweetest woman I've ever known, and I'm not saying that because she's my mother. I'm saying it because it's true. She was all of five feet tall, which was a stark contrast to my dad's 6'4" frame, but she was tough. My mother didn't drink or smoke or typically use choice words, but if you made her mad you were in trouble. When she got really ticked off she began her chastisement by saying, "Now let me tell you something." When mom loaded the car to take some of us with her she always turned to us and said quite clearly: "You better not show your asses." Mother was very loving and nurturing and taught us what we needed to know. She taught all of us – not just the girls – how to cook and properly maintain a household. She joined dad in stressing the importance of education. She taught my sisters what it meant to be a lady, and she taught my brothers and me how to treat a woman.

My mother always told me how smart and handsome I was because she knew the importance of high self-esteem for black children in the fifties, sixties and seventies. She was always very proud of us when we excelled in school. Equally important, she disciplined us when we needed it. She and my dad were firm believers in Proverbs 13:24: "He that spareth his rod hateth his son, but he

24

that loveth him chasteneth him betimes." The more common

translation is spare the rod, spoil the child.

My mom always prayed for me, and I'm sure in the weeks before

her death she talked to God about me often. She didn't love me more

than the others; she knew I was in trouble.

Like mothers of all races my mother sacrificed so I could get the

things I wanted. If she needed a new coat but I needed something for

school, the coat had to wait. If she wanted a new hat for church but I

wanted to go on a school field trip she wore an old hat instead. My

mother was a good woman on whom I could always count.

And Lord have mercy could she burn! When mom entered the

kitchen the cooking Gods joined her, and when she emerged we

knew we were in for a treat. My mother cooked breakfast, lunch and

dinner every day for umpteen years for her husband and children. Of

course she missed a meal here and there because we ate out

sometimes, and as we kids got older and left home she was able to

cook less. But suffice it to say Louise Strong kept her family well fed.

Sunday mornings were the best. I fondly remember smelling

sausage and ham as mom cooked while listening to her favorite gospel radio program. On some Sundays she hot combed my sisters' hair, but we always had special breakfasts on Sundays. Mother got up early and cooked breakfast for her crew every morning – despite going to work most mornings. She wasn't a stay-at-home mom; she was a do-it-all-mom. And after working hard all day for others, she came home and cooked for us. Dinner was special in the Strong household, and you had to have a damn good reason to miss it. It was a time for us to bond as a family and enjoy mother's culinary expertise. But dinnertime wasn't for idle chat or loud music. Our parents did most of the talking, and when we spoke we usually updated them and each other on how things were going in school. Sometimes when I think about how we all sat around the table enjoying our food and sharing with each other I lament the fact that such family time is practically a lost art today.

Anyway, I had a wonderful, beautiful, "prayed up" mother. And I had a good upbringing. My parents loved, respected and complemented each other. Ever have someone special in your life who just doesn't really know you, get you or feel you? My parents knew, got and felt each other. The love they shared set the relationship bar for my siblings and me. Their love helped us get off on the right foot as the old folk say. Their love was beautiful. Sure they had their ups and downs as do all couples, but what they had was real.

My parents loved each other and their children, and for that I am eternally grateful.

So I'm sure you're wondering with such wonderful parents and so much love how on earth did I become a drug addict.

Read on.

Chapter 3
My Childhood

I'm not one to make excuses and don't tolerate them well. Likewise, I don't constantly look for someone or something to blame. Even so, there's a reason drinkers start imbibing in the first place, and among them are peer pressure, a desire to fit in and depression.

I took my first drink at age eight. It sounds ridiculous, but when you grow up in a small South Carolina town and your father's a moonshiner who owns a nightclub it's really not so surprising. I remember once dad handed me a cup of his latest concoction. While standing beside his still he extended his arm, told me to taste his wares and could tell by my expression I liked it. I occasionally went with my dad to his still and vividly remember him pouring the moonshine through a felt hat to strain it. My dad was known for having some of the best moonshine around. His brother and three of his nephews worked with him, so I guess you could say it was a family business. But please don't misconstrue what I'm saying because I absolutely am not blaming dad for the way my life turned out. My dad was one of the best, hardest-working and most reliable men I've met. My only regret about him is I didn't get close to him sooner. The truth is I didn't start drinking heavily until I joined the Air Force. In high school I made excellent grades, was president of my senior class, was voted "Best All-Around and Most Talented," was the starting point guard on the varsity basketball team and earned MVP honors.

It's true I was "all that" in high school, but it's also true I started experimenting with alcohol and drugs before earning my diploma. I wasn't into anything too heavy, but like a lot of kids in the late seventies and early eighties I drank a little beer and liquor and tried weed. My drug use neither escalated to a point where I thought I had a problem – notice I said thought – nor kept me from graduating with honors and a very promising future. The reality is, however, my drug use during high school was more serious than I realized. It was more serious than I was willing to admit.

After graduating I joined the Air Force, which caught my mom and most of my siblings off guard. I didn't know a lot about the military but knew it could help pay for college and would be a good way to travel. I'd always wanted to travel, likely because I grew up in a small town that offered little in the way of excitement. My brother, Calvin, who was already in the Army at the time, suggested the Air Force because of my academic talents. When I left for basic training my dad hugged me good-bye at the bus station and said he loved me. I was eighteen, and it was the first time in many years my dad had said those words to me. As the bus rolled away from my hometown, I had no idea how dramatically my life was about to change.

I did basic training at Lackland Air Force Base in San Antonio, and it was the first time I'd been in the western U.S. After basic training I was sent to the nation's capital. Imagine a country boy who grew up on a farm and had only fifty or so people in his senior class and there I was standing on Fourteenth Street in Washington, D.C.! I grew wide-eyed as I took in the lights, people and hustle and bustle. I guess you could say I was like the country bumpkin in Stevie

Wonder's hit "Living for the City." When he became of age he left his hometown, hopped a bus to New York and once off the bus was mesmerized by The Big Apple's tall buildings and bright lights. When I look back on it the day I set foot in D.C. was the day my life really started changing – and not for the better.

So there I was standing on Fourteenth Street reading my orders when a little old lady approached me. She said I looked out of place and asked where I was going, so I showed her my papers mandating I report to a base in Alexandria, Va. She grabbed my hand, led me to the correct city bus, got on with me and told the driver where I was headed. He was nice enough to point out my stop, and I thanked the little old lady as I exited. I found the unit to which I was assigned and it was on! I made a beer run with the guys, which was a foreshadowing of things to come. When we got to the barracks we drank the beer and smoked some pot. That's right. I got high with colleagues and superiors on my first day in the Air Force. Drinking beer and smoking pot became a ritual in the barracks, and eventually I was introduced to a small portion of cocaine, which ultimately changed my life.

After twenty-six weeks I graduated with the necessary skills to be a lithographic technician, a job I thoroughly enjoyed and worked while stationed in Germany and Peru. As a testament to the way my parents reared us, I reported early for work and handled my responsibilities proficiently without abusing lunch breaks. I also stayed late when necessary and got along well with my co-workers. I was an employer's dream – except for my well-hidden substance abuse problem.

Remember career day at your elementary school? Everyone wanted to be a teacher, policeman, doctor, firefighter, astronaut or whatever – anything but an addict. Addiction happened gradually in my case. I began as a social drinker, having a few beers at company functions or while out with friends. Eventually a few beers became quite a few and soon I was drinking before and during work. I also started needing drugs more and more. I'll never forget at nineteen riding in a plane to Frankfurt, West Germany. After landing and taking a two-hour bus ride through The Eifel Mountains I arrived at my first duty station. My supervisor met me at the depot, and we went straight to a club to drink beer. I was a very good lithographic technician and took my job quite seriously, but soon I was drinking heavily every day and chasing just about every woman I laid eyes on. That dangerous, careless lifestyle continued during my two-year assignment in Germany.

Chapter 4

Marriage

Three years after I enlisted, I was home on furlough visiting one of my sisters when LaDonna sashayed in to "Juicy Fruit" by Mtume. As usual I was getting my drink on, and it was lust at first sight. Within a month LaDonna and I were married. A wise woman once said things that don't start out right probably won't end up right. Too bad she didn't reach me before I took the plunge. I arrived at the ceremony more than an hour late and I reeked of alcohol. Making matters worse I didn't love LaDonna. I knew I didn't love her but was determined to get married anyway.

I married LaDonna based on superficial feelings. She was extremely attractive, and I hadn't seen a black woman that beautiful in over two years while stationed in Germany. Thinking back on it, this was when the obsessive and compulsive behaviors that often accompany addiction began developing in me. I mean who gets married to someone after just a month? And even though I didn't love LaDonna, I constantly thought about her. It was all LaDonna all the time. But quiet as it's kept my life was already unmanageable from an emotional standpoint because my heart was taken by a beautiful Frau named Silvia who captured my heart, mind and spirit the first night we met at a popular nightclub in Trier, Germany. Silvia was beautiful and looked like Lynda Carter (Wonder Woman). When she motioned for me from across the room I had a hard time believing she was summoning me. At times I've been on top of the world and at other times I've struggled with low self-esteem. The emotional and mental strength I possess today are in stark contrast to my emotional makeup when I dated Silvia and subsequently married LaDonna.

While reflecting on those times now I can easily see the emotional patterns that were developing in my relationships. I always wanted to be in relationships but didn't know how to cope in them. This may seem like simple stuff to many men, but for me it was very tough. It was as though a part of me wanted to express my deepest feelings while another part said I shouldn't. This, I know now, was caused in part by misinformation gathered while growing up in a small, southern town where most men I knew with the exception of my dad rarely expressed their deepest feelings unless they were outraged, drunk or high. Unfortunately, my emotional instability helped destroy many of my early relationships. Anyway, soon after I began dating Silvia I received orders to return to the states. I was devastated over having to leave Silvia. You see what I thought was love for Silvia was actually obsession. I would have done just about anything to stay with her, but you can't fight Uncle Sam so I returned to the states desperately needing something to fill the void in my heart and LaDonna was it. I realize now it was so unfair to do that to LaDonna, who was living in South Carolina when I asked her to marry me. Initially we lived in Indiana, and in our first month of marriage she got pregnant. Within three months I was drinking and smoking weed heavily to try to suppress lingering feelings for Silvia. At some point during our first year of marriage I started cheating on LaDonna. One day when I was sober enough to realize the marriage was a mistake, I decided to ask her for a divorce. I wasn't ready to be faithful, wasn't in love with her and hadn't expected to become a father so soon. So one day after work I asked LaDonna for a divorce but she told me I wasn't going to get rid of her that easily. LaDonna really loved me, and we already had a son. I guess she felt I'd taken her from her home and be damned if she was going to just let me go.

Our son was a happy kid, but he didn't start talking or walking at the ages most kids do. I know children don't develop at the same pace, but I had a nagging suspicion something was wrong. I kept telling LaDonna we needed to take him to the doctor for a thorough checkup, but she kept saying he was fine. Finally I put my foot down and scheduled an appointment, and that's when we learned our son had lost more than seventy percent of his hearing because of an undetected ear infection. The poor little fella had to have tubes surgically inserted in his ears and eye surgery when he was only eighteen-months-old. Needless to say his health challenges added to the stress in our marriage, and I shamefully used that as an excuse to continue cheating. A few years after our son was born we had a daughter, but things weren't really any better between us. Eventually LaDonna left and I wound up back in my parents' house with our children. I was paying rent instead of just mooching off them, but before too long LaDonna returned to South Carolina and we got our own place. LaDonna and I really tried to make the marriage work, but too much damage had been done. Hell, we were just kids when we married – I was twenty-two and she was nineteen – and to our credit we stayed together for eight years. But one morning in 1990 I decided marriage was no longer for me. I was drinking more, and my addiction to cocaine was so bad I couldn't go a day without it. I was sneaking out to my car at night during work to drink booze and snort coke. The truth is I'd fallen completely out of love with LaDonna and had reconciled solely for the sake of the kids. Even so, I just couldn't stay married any longer. So I came home from work that night in 1990 and informed LaDonna of my decision to get a divorce. She wasn't happy but didn't put up much of a fight. I think deep down she knew it was over; however, I accept the majority of the blame for our failed marriage.

Chapter 5
Life After Marriage

After LaDonna and I split for good I moved back in with my parents – this time without my kids – and spent virtually every dollar I had on cocaine, alcohol and women. Eventually the madness that was my life became so overwhelming I quit my supervisor's job at the bearing manufacturing company and left South Carolina for The Big Apple. I landed a job at *The New York Daily News* and crossed the picket line to become a scab when employees went on strike. As a scab I was treated like royalty: Company executives put me in a plush hotel, paid me and gave me money for food. But everything wasn't golden. I once got hit in the chest with a brick thrown through a windshield, and on another occasion I was shot at by union workers. Yet neither of those incidents stopped me from being a scab. I worked that gig for about four months and spent the money I made on cocaine and alcohol. Needless to say I forgot all about the two children I left with their mom in South Carolina. As painful as this is to admit, it was like they didn't exist. What I didn't know then but realized over time is I was running from myself and from my feelings. The geographical changes and drugs anesthetized the feelings of inadequacy, low self-esteem and low self-worth that were beginning to consume me. The more I felt those feelings the more I didn't want to, so I just kept on getting high.

Eventually I left NYC and returned to South Carolina to live with my sister, Margaret. My addiction spiraled out of control and after a year I left South Carolina again, this time for Wilmington, Del. I landed a job as a collector for a national bank and did well enough to be recognized as one of the top performers in the organization, earning bonuses larger than my salary. Believe it or not during this time I took a break from drugs and drank mostly good cognac. My favorite was Courvoisier, straight with no ice or chaser because having cognac any other way is just uncivilized.

While I lived in Delaware I didn't keep in touch with my family as regularly as I should have, but I was aware mom had gotten sick again. Mom had diabetes and some other medical challenges, so at times her health wasn't the greatest. Because I wasn't communicating with my family regularly, I didn't realize just how bad things had gotten with her. So when I called my sister, Lisa, to check on mom I was beyond floored when my brother-in-law said somewhat incredulously, "Oh, don't you know? Your mother died this morning." I was pretty steamed at James for quite some time for telling me about mom's death that way, but in reality I was mad at myself for not being in touch with my family and for not being there for mom. Getting angry at my brother-in-law was my feeble attempt to blame him for my own shortcomings.

I told you in chapter two mom and dad never gave up on me. Well, many years after she died dad told me she prayed for me every single day. Call it a mother's intuition, but though I tried to conceal my addiction and alcoholism mom knew. Dad said she knew what was going on with me but always believed one day I would be all right. When mom died I was only twenty-nine. After hearing those words from my brother-in-law I was such a basket case my co-workers had to take me into a conference room to get me calmed down. It's hard enough to lose your mother under any circumstances, but compounding my grief was the guilt I felt over not being there for her. My mom knew I loved her, but sometimes loving a person isn't enough and you've also got to be there for that person. After I composed myself I went home. My co-workers had graciously booked and paid for my flight, so I didn't have to deal with that. Once I got home I got stoned out of my mind and contemplated suicide. In fact, I got dangerously close to a window that night but one of my buddies cursed me out and told me jumping wouldn't solve a damned thing and sure as hell wouldn't bring mom back.

After mom's death life was much the same for me until one night I ran into a young lady while walking to a corner store for cigarettes and alcohol. She asked me if I was looking, and the next thing I knew I was in a basement smoking cocaine and having sex with a strange woman. That night was the beginning of the end of my time in Delaware. I resumed smoking crack and eventually lost my job and apartment, and I was dating two women at church until the pastor politely asked me to leave and not come back. So here I was homeless, jobless and penniless again. In a moment of clarity I decided to visit my brother, C.C., who lived less than ninety minutes away in Baltimore. We weren't overly close growing up because he was much older and from dad's first marriage, so I saw this as the perfect opportunity to bond with him and familiarize myself with

Charm City. My first week there I landed a job at Citibank, and

before long I met a young lady and moved in with her. I was so very

lost when it came to women because I just didn't know what I

wanted or expected from them. I simply knew I needed them

because my self-esteem was incredibly low. Well, you can already

guess what happened. I starting using cocaine more heavily and I got

the young lady evicted, too. The women, musical chair jobs and drug

abuse became routine for me. Simply put, I was out of control and

clueless about how to free myself from the vicious cycle of

degradation, unemployment, addiction, self-loathing and no self-

respect. Despite my foolishness God blessed me with some very

good-paying jobs at The American Red Cross, Citigroup and Blue

Cross and Blue Shield. The sad thing is I always squandered them.

While millions of black men weren't getting the opportunities I got, I

was wasting them like nobody's business. They say a fool and his

money are soon parted. My name should have been Fool because I

kept getting good jobs and losing them. The constant in all of this

madness is there was always a strong black woman standing by to pick me up whenever I fell. Those strong, beautiful black women became my enablers during this dreadful time in my life.

Chapter 6

The Hunter

I've discussed never having trouble finding a woman for sex or to be my girl, but until now I haven't come clean about some of the women I got after my divorce and why I needed them. I haven't told you how my low self-esteem drove me to certain women and ultimately from them.

In this chapter I'll break it down, but to be clear I'm talking about my experience and not saying the way it was with me is the way it is for all brothers.

So what am I talking about? I guess you can call it gold-digger reversal. We all know women who prey on men with money, fancy cars and big houses. They're easy to spot unless you're wearing blinders. They dress to impress, are attractive, give a brother just enough attention to make him think he's the only man on earth and subtly interject money into conversations. Gold diggers are different from groupies who prey on professional athletes. They're all out for money, but groupies don't try to hide it. Gold-digger reversal refers to men who try to snatch women who've got it going on. I know a lot about this subject because after my divorce I participated in it.

This makes me sound trifling, but in my defense I wasn't a brother who lived off women. I've always worked and even snagged some good-paying jobs along the way. My reason for seeking highly successful women had nothing to do with an aversion to a nine-to-five and everything to do with low self-esteem. I was insecure about who I was, what I'd accomplished and my addiction. I was highly intelligent and dressed nicely, but neither my intelligence nor clothes could obliterate my insecurity. After years of suffering from low self-esteem I thought I'd discovered a way to improve it: date highly successfully, very attractive women.

I'd be having a brew with the fellas and all I wanted to talk about was my girl. How fine she was, how much money she made, how big her house was, what side of town she lived on, the fancy, invitation-only parties she got us into and the important people she knew. The more I talked and the more impressed the fellas seemed, the more my chest stuck out. Ever been there, brothers? Do you have a clue what I'm talking about? If not, I tip my hat to you because trust me when I say you don't ever want to be that brother. I wasn't mooching off these highly successful, very attractive women. Well, I guess it's fair to say I was mooching off their success. I was all caught up in their lives and accomplishments when I should have been trying to get my shit together. Instead of addressing what was going on internally and the reason I felt a need to always have highly successful, very attractive women in my life, I kept seeking successful women. In other words, I repeatedly masked the problem and tried convincing myself everything was everything.

Once I dated a sister who worked for the federal government, owned a bunch of property and made six figures. She said I didn't have to work and she would give me her car and keep money in my pocket. I didn't take her up on that, and it doesn't take Einstein to realize she clearly had some self-esteem issues, too. Her offer is indicative of how some women feel they have to buy their men, but that's not the point of this chapter.

We've all heard you can run but you can't hide. It should come as no surprise that though I had no problem finding and dating highly successful, very attractive women none of the relationships lasted. Even though my motive wasn't to mooch off them, sooner or later they realized they had it going on and I was going nowhere. Also, while I was lacking in self-esteem, I still had a healthy sense of dignity and eventually couldn't deal with the fact that I was the weakest link in the relationships. So I bounced or did something sufficient to make the women bounce. I seemed to always be in relationships but the reality is I never really wanted to be in committed relationships. I was an asshole back then, but the good news is eventually I came to grips with things and learned how not to be. I'm not glossing over this because my evolution from that is highly important, but I'll discuss how I changed later.

When I worked as a homeless shelter manager I encountered the man I used to be every single day. I saw brothers who checked in for two-month stays determined to find highly successful, very attractive sisters. That they were looking for these women at shelters may sound funny, but everyone in a homeless shelter isn't a vagabond. People go through trials and tribulations. They lose good-paying jobs because of company cutbacks. Their spouses or significant others swindle them out of their loot. They get sick and can't work. Trust me when I tell you there are a lot of successful women who temporarily end up at homeless shelters. And trust me when I tell you a lot of brothers go there hoping to end up with them. Instead of taking the allotted residence time to get back on their feet, land a job and start repairing their lives, many brothers go to shelters just to find women. That mentality infuriates me because even when I sought successful women I was a working brother whose reasons had more to do with low self-esteem than anything else. I'm not saying that made my actions okay, but I feel there's a difference. Some of the cats I'm referencing couldn't care less about employment. They viewed those women – who usually got back on their feet rather quickly – as meal tickets and pounced on them. I didn't realize it then but know now that although my motives for aligning with highly successful women weren't sinister, I was still being a sorry-ass brother.

Chapter 7
Baltimore

After my failed marriage and totally screwing up in Delaware, I moved to Baltimore to live with my brother, C.C. Getting a sister evicted was among several wrongdoings I committed in Charm City, and that woman wasn't the only person to get caught up in my mess. I dated quite a few women during the thirteen years I lived in Baltimore.

When I lived in Baltimore a few guys jumped me one night, putting me in the hospital for several days. Another time during a bar fight a beer bottle was smashed against my head. And one night I got so high I slipped and fell just as I reached the top step of my apartment. Fortunately I didn't break my neck, get seriously injured or suffer a concussion.

Those mishaps can't compare to other things I experienced in Baltimore. For example, I was in a crack house one night when a fellow addict got shot and killed at the front door. Yet nothing could have prepared me for what happened in May 2002.

It was fairly late on a Friday and I was counting the minutes 'til quitting time. It's one thing to look forward to the weekend but totally different when you're an addict and know two and a half days of getting high are about to commence. I was sitting at my desk thinking soon my girlfriend Lauren would be outside waiting on me because we'd made plans to go out for drinks. Lauren was a pretty heavy drinker and enjoyed having a good time, and in just minutes we'd be on our way to one of our favorite watering holes – or so I thought.

My reflections of a fun evening with Lauren were rudely interrupted by a telephone call from human resources. Before I continue, let me back up and tell you about my job at this time. I was a network administrator for The Baltimore City Health Department, and when I entered a room it wasn't uncommon for employees to start clapping because they knew network glitches were about to be fixed. Sometimes I'd be holed up for five or six hours trying to find the problem wire. The network administrator position afforded very little down time, but it paid more than sixty thousand dollars annually.

You may wonder how I landed such a good gig. Remember all of the hoopla about Y2K and the fears that at midnight on Dec. 31, 1999, computers would crash and send the world into a frenzy? The fallout was supposed to be maddening with lost medical records, hardened criminals being inadvertently released and planes dropping out of the sky. One day while checking the classifieds I saw a listing for a Y2K Specialist. I'd worked on computers extensively in The Air Force and knew about most of the old programs, and I'd also worked on systems supporting the Space Shuttle, so I applied. The man conducting the Y2K Specialist interviews was retired Navy. He took one look at my resume, asked a few questions to ensure I hadn't fabricated my skills and it was a wrap.

Anyway, back to that Friday. There I was minutes away from quitting time and getting my drink on with Lauren when HR called. In the past when I'd gone to the HR director's office to fix her computer we'd always talked and shared laughs, so I didn't hesitate to rib her about calling me so late in the day on a Friday. She ignored my little jokey-joke and very bluntly indicated I needed to come to her office ASAP, so I said okay and hung up. When I got to her office she told me to hold on a minute, and then she got up and walked out. Seconds later a man wearing a badge around his neck walked in. The moment I saw him I knew why I was there. Forget about the supposed Y2K crash. When I saw that badge my world came crashing down. You see, the whole time I'd been working for The City of Baltimore I'd been stealing computers from the health department, storing them at my crib and selling them to support my drug habit. So here I was forty years old and being charged with a crime for the first time in my life. My head was spinning, and my life flashed before me. What was I going to do? What would happen to me? How would I support myself? Was I headed to the pen?

The detective explained the charge without handcuffing me then discreetly escorted me to my desk where I quietly gathered my things and left. I'm sure some employees picked up on what was going down, but it could have been much more humiliating. Still, it was pretty bad. The HR director was too upset to hang around once the detective entered her office, and one of the ladies responsible for hiring me broke down and cried when she heard the news. Suffice it to say I hurt a lot of people.

And let's not forget about Lauren. By now it was past quitting time so she was already outside waiting. When she saw the dejected look on my face and box of personal items it took less than ten seconds for her to ask what was up. I couldn't tell the truth because of shame so I mumbled that I got fired because they said I stole some computers. Lauren asked point blank whether I'd stolen some computers and when I said yes she called me a stupid MF. Needless to say the rest of our night didn't go as planned, and it should come as no surprise our relationship was never the same.

I loved Lauren and really enjoyed spending time with her but had bigger fish to fry. Was I going to prison? Would I ever get another job? Bad news and good news ensued. I was fired from my job as a network administrator and blackballed from the profession, but when I went to court about a month later the judge was very lenient on me because I didn't have a rap sheet. He gave me six months of unsupervised probation and ordered me to pay restitution for the stolen computers.

No doubt I skated because many brothers have been sent up the river for much less. And it's not like I stole only one or two computers during the four years I worked for the city. My racket began shortly after I got hired and continued until one of my buyers got busted with a hot computer I'd sold him and ratted. It was quite an elaborate scheme to say the least. Nonetheless, even after receiving a tremendous break from the judge (I'm sure my mom was up in Heaven praying over me in the days leading up to my

sentencing) I still didn't straighten up. In fact, I started getting high

more often, and I continued my shenanigans with women. Lauren

and I continued seeing each other but eventually drifted apart. I

continued going down my self-destructive path of booze, drugs and

women.

I had no idea what lay ahead of me.

I was lost, dazed and confused.

Yet even though it hurt like hell at the time, getting fired from

The City of Baltimore was actually a blessing in disguise. Had I not

gotten caught I would have kept stealing, and there's no telling what

would have happened to me.

Chapter 8

August 22, 2002

Three months after getting fired I awoke on Aug. 22, 2002, in the basement of a crack house. With sleep still in my eyes and a dry mouth from a night of heavy drinking I asked myself how I'd gotten there. It was a valid question from a man who once aspired to be a doctor, lawyer or politician – anything but a junkie. Remember, I was president of my senior class, a champion public speaker, president of the United Methodist Council of Youth Ministries and voted "Best All Around and Most Talented." Likewise, I came from a close knit, loving family, once had a doting wife and in 1985 co-wrote one of the very first keypunch replacement programs for the Air Force. I had it all – until I threw it all away.

Yet as bad as things sound, Aug. 22, 2002, was actually a beautiful day. After thinking for a few seconds about my jacked-up life, a sense of calm gripped me. It was almost as though God was saying Michael, be still. On Aug. 22, 2002, I felt as though God was filling my heart with a willingness to change. It's one thing to know you need to change but another thing to do it. Nike made famous the phrase "Just Do It," but we all know it's hard to change. Consider the woman who's habitually late to work but continues setting her alarm for seven, the man who has trouble fitting into his clothes but refuses to diet or work out or the couple that has trouble communicating but won't consider counseling. We all need to change things about ourselves, but most of us resist change. For years I knew I needed to stop drinking and using drugs. Believe it or not one of my regular crack suppliers used to question my drug use. Granted he continued selling to me whenever I wanted to buy, but occasionally he'd say I didn't fit in as a junkie and was stupid for using. Maybe it was because when he saw me I was dressed to the nines, often copping on his corner after a day in the office. Or perhaps it was because I just didn't seem like an addict to him. Think of the irony here: A drug dealer, a man whose very livelihood depends on loyal customers like me, told me I needed to stop using. Like I said, I knew I needed to change but something just wouldn't let me. I knew addiction had helped destroy my marriage, alienated me from my family and friends and affected me in negative ways. Likewise, I knew every day I continued using I risked getting busted with coke, heroin or some other drug and going to prison. Even worse, I knew I could end up dead in a Baltimore alley, becoming just another statistic in a city infamous for its homicide rate. I knew, but I still didn't stop until Aug. 22, 2002.

There are so many people caught in the trap of recreational drug use. They begin by doing a line of coke at a swank party because it's the "in thing" to do and before long they're addicted. I sure was clueless about just how addictive drugs and pills could be when I began using. In the 1980s some black men began letting drugs rule their lives and lost their edge. I was so lost at one point my pastor in Wilmington, Del., told me drug use had depleted my manhood. Being arrogant and self-centered at the time, I simply shrugged off his comments. Truth be told I really didn't grasp what he meant back then but understand now without question. When substance abuse consumes your life, you stop striving to be your best through hard work, honesty and commitment. I never imagined where my recreational drug use would take me. I started experimenting with weed at an early age and by nineteen was taking acid, snorting coke, using heroin and popping pills.

And I wasn't alone. There were tens of thousands of brothers just like me but they lacked an educational or military background. More often than not they resorted to crime to make ends meet – not that I didn't break the law a time or two – but because of my

background I always managed to land good jobs and keep money in

my pocket.

During the late seventies and early eighties a monster known as

crack cocaine began rearing its ugly head in this country, particularly

in cities like Baltimore, Detroit, Little Rock, D.C., Atlanta, L.A. and

Chicago. Crack was far cheaper and easier to get than the powder

form of cocaine, being used mainly by rich people, and quickly

became the drug of choice in the hood. It also became my drug of

choice. Crack destroyed untold numbers of black families and took

over America's inner cities like Michael Jordan took over The NBA.

It ruled the streets like Tiger Woods rules golf courses. And it

dominated lives like Venus Williams dominates Wimbledon. Even

though it's true crack costs far less than powder cocaine, a racist law

passed in nineteen eighty-six – the catalyst for which was the

shocking, cocaine-induced death of Maryland Terrapins basketball

star Len Bias – meted much harsher sentences to those caught with

crack than its powder counterpart. That meant brothers who got

busted with crack were being sent up for long periods of time, which only exacerbated the decline of the black family. Remember, some addicts managed to hustle here and there, earning a little dough with which to buy food and clothes for their family, but I've yet to see the brother who can send money home from the pen.

I began using drugs heavily in the eighties and got high all the way into late two thousand and two. I cringe now just thinking about it, but on August 22, 2002, I awakened broken and funky and knew I'd had enough. You see despite all of my so-called friends, the women, sex and parties, on that day I felt alone. On that day I had an epiphany and realized my life needed to change.

So after accepting the peace that deluged me, I dragged myself off the dirty couch I'd been sleeping on for weeks and showered for the first time in a minute. I slipped into a pair of Cross Colors jeans, a Nike T-shirt and some white tennis shoes, raked through my hair, which by now resembled a fro, grabbed my pack of Newports, my three dollar, forty-seven cents life's savings and prepared to hop a city bus. I knew when I awakened that morning I was going to a treatment center. Of course as luck would have it, the woman whose basement I'd been slumming in was coming in the door as I was going out. Surprised to see me up and about, she asked where I was going while invitingly flashing a handful of drugs. I told her bluntly, "I can't get high no more." She looked at me, said okay and stepped aside. Most addicts like company while getting high, but she'd been on me for a while to get clean because she said using wasn't for me. It's funny how addicts tell others they shouldn't get high but won't tell themselves. Anyway, she moved aside and I left, taking my biggest steps since learning to walk.

Outside, the beginnings of a typical summer day were emerging. Normally my first thought would be to score some drugs, but I was so spiritually and emotionally broken I didn't want to get high. I wanted to get help.

I'd heard about different treatment centers but because I'm a veteran figured I should go to the VA Hospital on North Greene Street. (Incidentally, that's where I took the picture I referenced at the beginning of this book.) After having my ID made I was told to go to Maryland Center for Veterans Education and Training, or MCVET, ironically located on High Street.

At MCVET I twice started to turn and run. Remember what I said about change? By now I knew I desperately needed to change, but it was still hard for me to go inside MCVET. Going inside meant I had a problem, and it's not easy to admit you've got a problem. I finally mustered the courage to go inside, which as it turns out was only half the battle. I sat down in front of a female intake counselor who bluntly asked why I was there. When you abuse drugs and run the streets for more than 20 years you become quite adept at bullshitting, so in a lame attempt to camouflage the truth I fed her a line about being tired and needing a temporary place to rest. The sister looked right through me and repeated the question, this time addressing me by name. I tried to bullshit her again to no avail. So there we were involved in a pretty good staring contest because she knew she couldn't help me if I couldn't admit why I was there. When I finally accepted I'd hit rock bottom and this placed called MCVET was my last hope, I started crying. I was a grown man just months shy of forty-one, and I was crying like a baby in front of a stranger. But the harder I cried the freer I felt, and soon after my emotional outburst I said what I had denied for years: "I am a drug addict."

CHAPTER 9

MCVET

I'd never been in a treatment facility and didn't know what to expect, but I knew this placed called MCVET was my only hope. So after I broke down and cried while finally admitting I was a drug addict, the sister completed my admission forms. I don't recall every detail of the intake process but remember feeling pretty damned lost and very hopeless. I had no clue what was in store for me or how long I'd reside at this place called MCVET, but somehow I knew it's where God wanted me to be.

MCVET is structured like the military, and initially I was assigned to first platoon on the first floor and slept on the top bunk while "Da Hawk" slept below. Eventually I transitioned to second platoon on the second floor. During both stages I slept in an open bay with forty other guys.

My first few weeks at MCVET were rough – especially while I went through detoxification. A lack of cocaine doesn't cause physical withdrawal, so I wasn't constantly shaking, throwing up or hallucinating like you see in movies. I experienced mental detox. At night I stayed awake in a cold sweat thinking about getting high. My sleeping patterns didn't adjust for at least two months, and I was constantly nervous and emotional. I really had no idea just how emotionally screwed up I was until I decided to stop doing drugs. As strange as it may sound, I went through a grieving process. It was as if someone dear to me had died or left my life forever. I just wasn't sure I could function without drugs and alcohol, and I was depressed.

It should come as no surprise I was ashamed to be in treatment. Not me, the kid voted "Best All Around and Most Talented." Not the guy who helped write one of the first keypunch replacement programs for the Air Force. Not the man who only three months prior was pulling down more than sixty thousand dollars a year in a highly respectable job. Rehab? Adding insult to injury we had to get up every day at five a.m. to police the area around the building, and while picking up trash I'd see former health department co-workers driving by. They saw me picking up trash along Gay Street, which made me wonder whether that's how inmates feel when they're collecting trash along the highway. We weren't wearing neon vests, but my former colleagues knew what time it was. Humiliating? No question. Yet I came to realize God was preparing me for a life without drugs and a relationship with Him.

I mentioned I was depressed. I was also mad at myself. I told you I used to have an over-inflated ego. I would look at the people around me and convince myself I was better than them because I always landed pretty decent jobs. During periods of intense denial I told myself I wasn't a junkie, and I even started believing the hype. But now here I was, just months removed from that sweet network administrator job, and the reality that I was a drug addict was finally setting in. So anger was mixed in with my other emotions.

My anger didn't last long thanks in part to the acceptance I immediately received from Eddie, Keith and Steve. Those brothers were a Godsend. They'd all been in treatment before and encouraged me and told me things I needed to know. They treated me like the rookie on an NBA or NFL team. Old Mike would have turned his nose at them and figured if they really knew anything they wouldn't be in rehab again, but I listened to them and tried to learn from them, which signaled progress and maturity. Interestingly, during my first two weeks at MCVET three guys asked me to keep their money in my locker. It seemed everyone knew I was still pretty honest, and whenever some of the guys and I talk today they always say I had a look that said I wouldn't steal from them.

But back to my first few days. I was embarrassed when I stood in class to introduce myself, disclose my military branch and say why I was there. But I got through it. The next day, on Aug. 23, 2002, I attended a class taught by James Metts. Mr. Metts was a counselor who whipped us into shape and helped us understand just how badly we'd screwed up.

Unlike any man I'd met, he was a heavily decorated sharpshooter who was sent to Vietnam to fight for his country at eighteen. During class Mr. Metts discussed his missions and drug use while overseas. It's no secret a lot of American soldiers used drugs heavily while in 'Nam. The reported drugs of choice were marijuana and heroin, and many servicemen returned home with substance-abuse problems. Mr. Metts talked about his time in Vietnam but primarily discussed how to transition from being hopeless dope fiends to happy, normal people and what that meant.

At one point Mr. Metts was a homeless, down-and-out drug addict, so he wasn't just talking the talk but had walked the walk. And he didn't mince words. At one time he was a self-proclaimed "bottom feeding dope fiend." But Mr. Metts overcame his substance abuse problems, got his GED, enrolled in a community college and eventually transferred to a four-year institution before earning bachelor's and master's degrees in social work.

Mr. Metts was the first man to look me directly in the eyes and kick it to me straight. I can't speak for the other addicts sitting in the classroom, but his words carried a ton of weight for me because he'd been there and done that. Over the years I've heard many people talk about drug abuse and the ills it spawns, and Lord knows there have been countless dollars spent on examining the problem of homelessness in this country. But many of the people talking about substance abuse and homelessness don't know the first thing about either. They've done research and gathered statistical data, but as the

69

saying goes experience is the best teacher. Mr. Metts had plenty of experience and knew his stuff.

Even though it's been more than eleven years, I vividly remember walking into his classroom on Aug. 23, 2002, because Mr. Metts immediately jumped on me. Gazing at me with a look of disgust, he said it was a shame a grown man was in a recovery house expecting other people to take care of him and I couldn't blame anyone but me for my circumstances. Until that point I'd never critically examined myself. I'd masked my feelings for so long with sex, drugs and alcohol 'til I truly didn't know who I was or how I fit in with the world. During the two decades I got high I had some beer, wine, liquor, champagne, reefer, cocaine, heroin or pills every, single day, and on most days I had a combination of substances. I also kept a woman around and sometimes more than one. So when I say I masked my feelings with sex, drugs and alcohol that's exactly what I mean. I'd become so important to myself and so self-centered it was all about Michael. During the eighties and nineties I worked, got high and chased women. That was my life in a nutshell. All the while I was missing out on my children's lives, a mistake for which I've finally forgiven myself.

Yet here was this man challenging me and saying my messed-up life was my fault. He wasn't worried about hurting my feelings. He was giving it to me straight and telling it like it was.

Mr. Metts didn't mince words and also had a way with words. He didn't speak perfect grammar or use the biggest words in the dictionary, and he didn't preach Einstein's Theory of Relativity. Mr. Metts shot from the hip without sugarcoating things. I'll never forget him looking at me and saying I was a steaming pile of shit and a waste of skin. Imagine someone saying you you're a waste of skin? But that wasn't all. Mr. Metts asked if a woman got involved with me what would she tell her father. With a serious look on his face he mocked me and said "Daddy, I met and fell in love today with a man who has absolutely nothing." Ouch. That really hurt; especially given I'd always considered myself a real catch. Mr. Metts' words cut to the bone because I was almost forty-one with nothing to show for myself. I didn't own a car. I certainly didn't own a home. And I'd checked into MCVET with three dollars and forty-seven cents to my name. I had nothing because I'd foolishly squandered it all away.

No one had ever verbally kicked my ass or emasculated me like Mr. Metts. He wasn't afraid to say what was on his mind, and I can't tell you how much I admired him for that. In those moments when he pretty much told me I was worthless, instead of wanting to fight him I wanted to be like him. I knew if Mr. Metts could overcome his addiction, obtain college degrees and admit to others what he used to be, I could do it too – or so I hoped.

Needless to say Mr. Metts' presence and the class he taught made all the difference in the world to me. I'm not saying I wouldn't have survived at MCVET without him, but his impact on me was profound. I started looking forward to his classes and being grateful to be in treatment. As the days turned into weeks and the weeks turned into months, I began realizing how good MCVET was for me. I was learning to exist without drugs and alcohol. I was taking a long, hard look at myself and coming to grips with what I saw. I was accepting responsibility for my life and no longer blaming others. And I was slowly but surely starting to envision a day when I'd rejoin society as a productive member – not as a no-good addict who wasn't worth the time of day.

Chapter 10

Getting Adjusted At MCVET

I meant it when I said I was beginning to picture a day when I rejoined society as a productive member, but I knew that wouldn't happen overnight. I had a good job just three months before checking into MCVET, but I hadn't been a productive member of society for a long time. Productive members of society own cars, don't steal from their employers and don't work solely for get-high money. Productive members of society take care of their kids and don't need drugs, alcohol and women to feel important. So even though I started fantasizing about returning to a normal life, I was under no illusion of being ready to make that move. In fact, though it's sad to admit, MCVET was the first place that felt like home to me in quite some time. A place I'd never set foot in, filled with people I'd never seen and decorated with furniture and artwork I didn't choose felt like home. I guess it's not so strange though because at MCVET I could be me. It wasn't South Carolina where whenever I went back home I acted as though everything was just fine. It wasn't the health department where I consciously watched what I said so I wouldn't let on that I was an addict and stealing from the company. At MCVET there was no need to be fake. Although I wasn't happy with who I was, at MCVET I could start dealing with my reality.

I told you earlier about getting up at five to police the area outside MCVET. Well, that was the least of our duties. First platoon resembled basic training and was the toughest part of MCVET's program. I guess they intentionally made it tough to weed out the men and women who lacked the mental, physical and spiritual fortitude to stay the course. We also had to perform kitchen patrol, latrine detail, guard duty and undergo twice-daily formations, and residents weren't allowed to go anywhere without having their movements documented. For instance, if I went to a bank I had to have the bank employee who handled my transaction sign my MCVET-issued pass. My life was in the hands of someone else the whole time I was in first platoon. It was humiliating to say the least and reminiscent of hall passes in middle school, but as the saying goes you make your bed...

Before too long I graduated to transitional housing and could come and go as I pleased as long as I was back by the ten thirty curfew. During transitional housing I spent most of my time in group therapy or employment and training counseling. I was also interviewed by my case manager and I attended a ton of meetings. After ninety days I was allowed weekend passes twice a month.

The maximum length of time in transitional housing is two years. Some people stay the entire twenty-four months; others don't. In transitional housing I was given the opportunity to return to work or go to school. Before I tell you what I chose, let me tell you something amazing that happened shortly after I arrived at MCVET.

I told you Mr. Metts ripped into me from day one and didn't let up. Well, he also recommended me for platoon leader. Looking back, I realize Mr. Metts saw potential in me that I didn't. By the time I got to MCVET Mr. Metts had been in the trenches long enough to know you can't save everybody. He would have given just about anything for a one hundred percent success rate but knew some of us would return to a life of drugs and alcohol. Mr. Metts knew some of us would be junkies for life, so I guess it's fair to say he saw some real promise in me.

His recommendation came as a huge surprise! I'd been captain on my high school basketball team and teachers often called on me for answers in high school, but those days were long gone and this was serious business. Platoon leader wasn't just a catchy title to make a recovering addict feel good. Platoon leaders at MCVET were responsible for the well being of fifty men. You'll recall when I checked into MCVET I could barely take care of me – much less fifty men. Now here I was just several months later getting the help I so desperately needed and being recommended for platoon leader.

Mr. Metts' recommendation was accepted, and I became responsible for making appointments for the men, assigning housekeeping duties to them and handing out disciplinary actions. I was also responsible for the platoon's overall appearance. The position helped me begin to find myself, regain my self-confidence and realize I didn't need to align myself with highly successful, very attractive women. Being platoon leader was extremely good for me.

It should come as no surprise there were some haters in the group of men I oversaw. I could tell some of the guys weren't happy I was put in charge of our group, but eventually the pettiness grew and I overheard guys whispering about plans to catch me in the bathroom and mess me up. Fortunately the guys were all talk and nothing bad happened to me during my three-month stint as platoon leader.

Remember I alluded earlier to a choice between returning to work and going to school? God blessed me to do both. The platoon leader position paid a small stipend, and I landed a job in the mailroom at Bank of America. I also won a scholarship at a local community college to obtain a certification in network systems.

The platoon leader position, the mailroom job and college scholarship were the beginning of my journey to real life. For the first time in my adult life I was conducting myself responsibly. I was beginning to realize life was so full of opportunities but it was up to me to seize them. Equally important, I was beginning to realize it didn't matter whether I succeeded at everything I tried. What mattered was I was learning how to react to success and failure, triumphs and disappointments, joy and pain. In "Can You Stand the Rain" by New Edition they sing about storms. I realize they're talking about relationships, but the same rule of thumb applies in life. I was learning everything wouldn't always go my way, and I was learning how to deal with negativity without resorting to drugs, alcohol and women.

While still living in transitional housing I took a network engineering course at Morgan State University. Eventually I graduated to single room occupancy and finally had my own room. I began a new job at Bank of America, my salary nearly tripled and things were really starting to look up. Before long I found myself repairing my credit, paying back taxes and catching up on my child support – things responsible adults do. When I got entangled in the world of drugs, alcohol and women my life completely changed and I was no longer a traditional member of society. The fact is I had no use for society as you know it – as I've come to know it. I played by Michael's rules and did exactly what I wanted. It was all or nothing with no gray areas, and when I made a decision I stuck to it. The problem was most of the decisions I made were usually bad and later bit me in the butt.

There were a lot of brothers like me back then who lost their way in a life of drugs, alcohol and women and weren't conforming to societal norms. They were doing exactly as they pleased and didn't give a damn about the consequences. When you're strung out you just really don't care. When you're on an airplane and the flight attendant demonstrates the safety instructions she always says put your mask on first if you're traveling with a small child or person requiring help. She says that because if you can't help yourself, aren't taking care of yourself and don't love yourself, there's no way you can adequately help, take care of or love someone else. Like George Benson says, learning to love yourself is the greatest love of all. While living at MCVET, I learned how to help, take care of and love me.

Chapter 11
Goodbye, Dad

While still at MCVET I took one of the most important, profound and special trips of my life. I didn't fly to Africa to bond with my brothers and sisters in The Motherland, venture to China to walk along The Great Wall or jet to Paris for a romantic rendezvous with a long-lost love. I flew to Charlotte, N.C., en route to Cheraw, S.C., to see my dad for the first time in almost three years. And I flew home to see him clean! I was high the last time my dad saw me, and the time before that, and the time before… You get the picture. But on July 13, 2004, I'd been living at MCVET for just under two years and was headed home for a much-needed, long overdue reunion with my dad.

It's less than eight hours from Baltimore to Charlotte by car, so the flight wasn't long. My baby sister Libbie picked me up and I was happy to see her, but my excitement over seeing her couldn't compare to what I would experience the next morning.

After Libbie picked me up we drove to the home of our sister Shawn and her husband Glenn. We ate fish and cabbage for dinner, and I really enjoyed spending time with family members whose faces

I hadn't seen in quite some time. I spent the night with Libbie and slept in a very nice guest bedroom, but it really wouldn't have mattered if I'd been staying at the Ritz-Carlton because my uneasiness about seeing dad the next morning made it hard to sleep.

Libbie and I got up early the next day and hit the road after our morning coffee. I enjoyed talking to her during the ninety-minute drive to Cheraw, S.C., where our dad was living in a nursing home. It's always nice catching up, and since I'd checked into MCVET I hadn't done a great job of keeping in touch with my family. I'm not making excuses, but I wanted to ensure things were working out at MCVET before announcing I was in rehab, so I just didn't contact my family for a minute. Anyway, despite the engaging conversation Libbie and I had on that short drive, foremost on my mind was seeing my dad.

Men, I don't know about you but even as I grew older, got married and started my own family I was still somewhat intimidated by my dad. He wasn't mean, but he also didn't mince words or have time for foolishness. I remember the day he caught me smoking outside our house while I was still in high school. He didn't make a big deal of it but instead told me I thought I was grown. Remember my dad was 6'4". Add to that the fact that I was the youngest of the six boys, and I guess I just always felt a little intimidated by him.

My dad and I had a pretty good relationship and never really got into any major arguments. But we didn't have the warm, close relationship I longed for. I knew my father loved and cared for me and would always protect me, but we just weren't as close as I would have liked. For example, when my dad hugged me good-bye at the bus station just before I left for the Air Force and told me he loved me, that was the first time in many years I'd heard him say those words.

My mind was racing as I rode with Libbie to dad's retirement home. Would he be glad to see me? Would we have anything to say to each other? Would I get bogged down in some of the not-so-good feelings from the past and ruin our time together? Would dad bring up the fact that I wasn't there for mom as I should have been during her last days? How would he look given he was in declining health?

I was both excited and nervous about seeing dad. I'd asked Libbie not to tell him I was coming because whether our visit was good or bad I wanted to surprise him. Unfortunately Libbie told our sister, Lisa, who is like a bucket filled with holes and can't hold water. So dad knew I was coming, which spoiled my surprise but by no means lessened the importance of my visit.

When we arrived at the retirement home dad was sitting on the patio. Much to my joy and great relief he was so very happy to see me. With a big, proud smile he told the retirement home staff several times that I was his son from Maryland. I never knew how proud dad was of me until that day. I realized as we talked many of the negative feelings I'd had about him could have been dealt with years earlier had I simply met with him sooner. But on July 14, 2004, I didn't lament what should have or could have been. I happily soaked in every precious second with my dad, who I'd always loved and who had always loved me despite our differences. I realized that day my dad had peace and love in his heart. He didn't admonish me for the years I missed with our family or sit there in his wheelchair and make feel bad, stupid or ashamed about being a recovering addict. And he didn't compare me to my siblings, most of whom are quite successful. Dad talked to me like a man who loved his son. He talked to me man to man.

I mentioned dad was in a wheelchair. By now at eighty-five he was fighting a physical battle but was armed with spiritual strength. I thought seeing him in a wheelchair would be hard, but the truth is he exuded so much peace and serenity the wheelchair became almost invisible to me.

As you've probably gathered, dad and I had a wonderful visit. During our reunion he told me how mom prayed for me every night, and he told me several times he was proud of me.

I told dad how I'd made a mess of my life with drugs and alcohol and that I was at MCVET piecing my life back together. As I talked about various bad situations I'd been in, dad listened quietly and patiently. When I took a break he told me something that stays with me. Remember my father made moonshine and owned a nightclub. I knew he drank and smoked cigarettes and cigars over the years, but I didn't know he went cold turkey one day. Dad stopped drinking and smoking on the same day and never looked back. After I finished talking about the mess I'd made of my life, dad looked at me in a loving, non-judgmental way and said, "Son, I haven't had a drink of liquor or a cigar in over thirty-two years. But this morning I had the taste for both a cigar and a drink." Dad said I was going to always have the taste for liquor, beer and other substances but I didn't have to have them. Wow. Sitting right in front of me was a great example of how to stop drinking and using drugs. And on a lot of days that conversation with dad helps keep me clean.

Dad and I ate some Mounds, his favorite candy bar, and chatted about many things until he grew tired. I could have sat in that nursing home talking to him all day but was mindful of his need for rest. Little did I know the next day would be the last time I'd see dad alive or speak to him. The last thing he said to me was, "Son, I love you. I love all of you."

Dad passed away a month later on Aug. 14, 2004. I thank God for allowing me to see dad before he died and for allowing me to be clean and in a really good place when I visited him. I'm eternally grateful for getting to hug and kiss dad and tell him I love him. I'm glad I got to mend the fences that for years had stood between us. That last visit with dad was a point of freedom for me because it erased any lingering resentment on my part. John Quincy Strong was my dad, and I realized he had learned the greatest of all of God's principles: unconditional love. He had learned it and lived it.

Michael Strong

After dad's funeral my brother-in-law, Glenn, commended me for delivering the eulogy and asked how I could do it. I told Glenn it was easy to talk so eloquently about dad. Sure I was hurting, but dad was a good man who loved his wife and kids and took care of them. My dad didn't make excuses but instead did what had to be done. He was a good man who practiced unconditional love, and I will love and miss him forever.

Chapter 12

Life After MCVET

Things continued going well at MCVET. I missed dad a lot but was at peace knowing I'd visited him and made things right between us. All was good with my job at Bank of America, and most importantly I was growing stronger spiritually, mentally, emotionally and physically. I knew I'd one day leave MCVET and it wouldn't be easy because I'd developed close relationships and become comfortable there. Even though the thought of re-acclimating to mainstream society didn't frighten me, I still had slight reservations about leaving.

Friends are the family we choose, and l chose several family members at MCVET. My fifteen siblings and I looked out for each other growing up, and I'm still grateful for my brother, Calvin, advising me to join the Air Force and for my brother, Jerome, telling me it's important for men and women in relationships to be friends and really like each other. My siblings and I had each other's backs in the usual ways, but having someone's back in recovery can mean life or death.

The bond between MCVET alumni is very strong. The relationships I formed with Terry C., Charles A., Dotson C., Keith D., Moreno R., Larry P., James H. and Willie B. remain intact today. We were our brothers' keepers at MCVET then and still are now.

Men don't usually share intimate thoughts with each other, which I think stems in part from being taught as boys that real men work through their problems alone and seeking help is a sign of weakness. Bullshit. Real men recognize when they need help and get the help they need. At MCVET we guys shared everything because recovery taught us keeping things bottled inside does more harm than good.

Leaving MCVET was always in the back of my mind though I wasn't chomping at the bit to go. Turns out Bank of America needed me to relocate to Phoenix, Las Vegas or Greensboro, N.C. I'd been to Phoenix while in the Air Force and loved it, but now that I'd gotten clean and begun repairing my life I knew I desperately needed to rebuild my relationship with my daughter, son and siblings. So after asking my daughter how she'd feel about me living two hours away in Greensboro, I left MCVET after three years and moved to North Carolina. I resumed working for the bank and before long purchased a car and my first home. I have to admit closing on my house was surreal. I once slept on a dirty couch in the basement of a crack house, and now I owned a home.

Michael Strong

Things were going well in the Tar Heel state, and I was slowly repairing my relationships. But every day is a struggle for addicts, and although I didn't get to North Carolina and start using again I made some unwise choices that cost me my job and my home. Suicidal thoughts emerged after the foreclosure, but I called my sponsor who told me to hold on. Though I felt there was nothing to hold on to, I took Tony G.'s advice. I also moved into his spare bedroom. I'd done so well at MCVET but now was broke and homeless again. Given my prior conviction for grand theft I didn't see a good job coming my way anytime soon. I started washing windows and eventually landed a job mopping and buffing floors at Food Lion. Needless to say I was experiencing a much-needed dose of humility, but that was okay. I realized I didn't need a hot job and that being human meant I was subject to shortcomings, mistakes and missteps. I worked those jobs, swallowed my pride, accepted my situation and sought solutions. I didn't get stuck in a rut or blame others but instead kept working the gigs I had until a better one came along.

Humility alleviated a ton of pressure and helped me realize I'm just plain 'ole Mike. I'm not saying it gave me a green light to constantly make mistakes, but it let me know it was normal to occasionally mess up because I'm human.

Losing my job and home was rough, but I got through it with the help of the God of my understanding. Landing a part-time job at Greensboro Urban Ministry was a big reason I survived. I didn't work part-time long before being offered a full-time job as their homeless shelter manager. I arrived at least thirty minutes early for work, rarely took lunch breaks and often stayed past quitting time. I revamped the company's computer system and quickly made a difference at Greensboro Urban Ministry. Managing the homeless shelter was right up my alley because I'd been homeless and could easily relate to the tenants.

The people at the shelter were desperately trying to turn around their lives. They weren't all addicts but many were, and I often told them I was an addict to give them hope.

It's hard to describe just how fulfilling it was to work at Greensboro Urban Ministry and help people in whose shoes I used to walk. I guess it's like a young boy who grows up without a father but later becomes one and teaches his son things his father didn't teach him. Or a convict who gets released from prison and lectures kids on making smart choices to avoid the pen. That I was helping people whose lives mirrored my former life meant more to me than just about anything. God had brought me out of the hell that was my life and put me in a job where I could make a difference. I'd had several jobs since Aug. 22, 2002, but the job at Greensboro Urban Ministry was so fulfilling.

While working at Urban Ministry I also worked as the weekend homeless shelter manager at Faith Step Ministries, a small, non-denominational church. And I re-established a much-needed, close personal relationship with God. Since I've been getting to know God I've found Him to be loving and caring and not the fire and brimstone God to whom I was introduced so many years ago. The God I trust and rely on lives inside my heart and soul.

I'd been visiting several churches since moving to North Carolina and after much deliberation and prayer joined Faith Step, which was attractive to me for many reasons. At Faith Step Sunday morning wasn't a fashion show, you didn't have to drive a luxury vehicle or make big bucks to join and there was no forty-five member choir. Most importantly our pastor, a woman I might add, taught the word.

I became comfortable enough at Faith Step to organize a men's group, and my faith grew tremendously through my relationship with God, my close friendship with Faith Step's pastor and my church involvement. I began going to God with things I used to worry about, and I was practicing the serenity prayer. I was learning to let go and let God, and what a relief that was. My relationship with God and my newfound faith had propelled me into a never-ending stream of hope. I'm not talking about hoping your team wins the Super Bowl or National Championship, or hoping for a raise. I'm talking about a profound, life-impacting hope. For me, HOPE became an acronym for Hang on Peace Exists.

Chapter 13

Prosperity

I loved my job at Greensboro Urban Ministry and was involved with a fairly active NA home group. I also met a recovering addict named Don, who was small in stature but big on life. A Philly native, he lived in Reidsville, about thirty minutes from Greensboro. What most attracted me to Don was his penchant for keeping it real – just like Mr. Metts. We hit it off and before long I asked him to be my sponsor. He accepted and I amicably parted ways with Tony G. While I lived in Greensboro a considerable number of people asked me to sponsor them and at one point I had no less than ten sponsees.

Things were going well in North Carolina but there was room for improvement. I told you I've forgiven myself for the precious time I missed from my children's lives, but that doesn't mean my former lifestyle didn't come with a price.

It did. It's hefty. I'm still paying.

Even though my daughter was amenable to my relocation, she didn't turn cartwheels over the news. We started getting closer when I moved to Greensboro and thankfully are much closer than we were just four or five years ago. There's still some pain and guilt associated with my former lifestyle, but the silver lining is we've grown closer during the past few years. I'll never forget the way she ran and jumped into my arms when I arrived unannounced at her job on Christmas Eve 2009. My daughter is twenty-six years old and the mother of a young son, but she literally ran to me with a huge smile on her beautiful face exclaiming, "Daddy, Daddy!"

I will continue fostering a close, loving relationship with my daughter, but I'm careful not to do too much to make up for my prior shortcomings. In other words, I'm not trying to buy my daughter's love. She's a single mom who works and supports a child, so I help her without overcompensating. And though I wasn't there for her when she was younger, I don't cut her slack when she messes up or let her guilt trip me. Through my recovery I've learned people must acknowledge their mistakes. If I bail out my daughter every time she messes up I'd be less than a father and wouldn't be teaching her accountability.

I took that same approach with the men and women at the Urban Ministry shelter. So many of them, particularly the men, were filled with excuses and blamed others for their messed-up lives. Sound familiar? I'd played the blame game long enough to see it coming a mile away and by the time I got clean and back on my feet had little tolerance for it. Don't get it twisted. I didn't become self-righteous, but I always checked brothers and sisters at the shelter when they started going down that road.

I loved my job and was beginning to feel at home at Faith Step. I had made a considerable number of friends in North Carolina and enjoyed being so close to my siblings. I didn't think twice about driving to South Carolina after work on Fridays to join my sister, Lisa, her husband James and their daughter, Jasmon, at a high school football game. And from time to time I'd find myself standing on the front porch of the home where I rented a room simply marveling at how far I'd come. Things were going well, but none of us knows what paths our lives will take. Around my three-year mark at Urban Ministry life took a turn I still find hard to believe.

One day while online, I saw a position at a treatment facility that sounded pretty good. I applied and was invited for an interview. My interview was on a Tuesday, lasted only thirty minutes and went extremely well. I spoke in an even tone and neither rushed my answers nor slowly gave them. I was careful not to appear cocky to the four interviewers, acknowledged I lacked experience in a few of the job's requirements and mentioned I was a quick study. I contained my excitement as I left but had a really good feeling about it. Less than forty-eight hours later my suspicions were confirmed when a woman called to offer me the job. Salary, benefits, vacation and the work schedule had been discussed during the interview, so I quickly accepted the offer without asking for time to think about it.

On June 17, 2010, I accepted the intake outreach coordinator position at MCVET! Can you believe it? I was hired to work at the very place where I spent three years of my life getting clean. When I walked through MCVET's doors on Aug. 22, 2002, I was a broken-down drug addict on his last leg. Hell, truth be told I was on my last foot. I left MCVET in 2005 to relocate to North Carolina and now was headed back as an employee!

Join the club if you're tripping because five years after I left MCVET as a recovering addict I returned as an employee. I was amazed, too, particularly during my first few days on the job. The rush I felt when I walked through MCVET's doors as an employee on July 6, 2010, is pretty indescribable. I got clean at MCVET, and though I'd been a faithful son and returned every year for Alumni Day I never imagined returning as an employee. Through the grace of

God I returned to the very place where I turned around my life.

Before I expound on my job at MCVET and being back in

Baltimore, I'd like to talk about my son so please bear with me.

Chapter 14

My Son

In the last chapter I briefly discussed my relationship with my daughter. In chapter four I mentioned my son, but I haven't told you everything there is to tell about him.

Perhaps I've waited until deep in this book to discuss him in detail because some things are just harder to deal with than others.

I love my son just as much as I love my daughter, but I still grapple with some intense feelings concerning him.

Michael DeMarkco Strong was born at 6:19 p.m. on Monday, Aug. 6, 1984, at Dukes Memorial Hospital in Peru, IN. LaDonna and I called him Markco from the beginning.

We had agreed to postpone having children until after LaDonna finished college, so when she informed me she was pregnant just three months into the marriage I wasn't happy. I was only 23 and not ready to be a father, but as time passed and I watched her stomach grow bigger my disappointment over the timing of her pregnancy gave way to excitement. In fact, as the months passed I started warming up to the idea and even went out and bought a handmade cradle for the little fella.

Aug. 6, 1984, was one of the happiest days of my life. I won't lie and say I had completely forgotten about our agreement to postpone having children, but I was very happy that day.

I smile when I reminisce about rocking Markco to sleep in my arms or sitting next to his cradle and watching him sleep. When he was only two-months old I bought him a pair of Nike tennis shoes and a Nike sweat suit because I was determined to have the best-dressed, most handsome two-month-old on this planet!

Unfortunately, Markco had it rough from the beginning and the doctor had to use forceps to get him out. And not too long after he was born I received orders to go to school in Rantoul, Ill. I don't know why but around this time I started feeling disconnected from my son, my family and my responsibilities as head of household. I was using at the time but I love my son so that wasn't it.

After my time in Rantoul I was given follow-up orders to move to Dayton, Ohio, and that's when things got really confusing and disappointing. When we moved to Dayton Markco was almost eighteen-months-old but was barely talking. After I finally convinced LaDonna we needed to take him to a doctor, we learned about his severe hearing loss and need for eye surgery. The news caused more emotional disconnect for me. Right or wrong, I was having a hard time accepting he was never going to be a normal kid. When my son needed me most, I wasn't there for him emotionally. We've all seen movies depicting parents with a really sick child and the stress that brings. I didn't bail on LaDonna because of our son's health problems, but the disconnect I felt toward him was very troublesome for me.

I credit LaDonna for being the rock and for being strong when I couldn't. Markco may have sensed he didn't get everything he needed from me, but I'm certain he knew how much love and attention he always got from his mom.

At some point LaDonna and I sent Markco to the South Carolina School for the Deaf and Blind, where he thrived and did as well as he could.

Two years after Markco was born we had Sade. But after eight years of trying to make things work LaDonna and I got divorced. Couples call it quits every day, but divorce is no excuse for not being there for your kids. My parents were each on their second marriage when they wed, but dad remained a good father to the children he had before marrying mom. Unfortunately after the divorce I didn't follow his lead. I started using drugs more heavily and basically forgot my children existed. I returned to South Carolina to visit them occasionally, but I wasn't in their lives by any stretch. Unbeknownst to me Markco was diagnosed with autism at age thirteen, something I learned eight years later when he was twenty-one. I'm sure some of you reading this are calling me trifling and other choice names. Believe me there's nothing you can say that I haven't already said.

You probably wonder whether I feel guilty about being so uninvolved in Markco's life. I don't think about it every day, but it comes to mind often enough. Do I wish I'd hung around to ensure he received the very best medical care? Absolutely. I'm not implying LaDonna didn't see about his medical needs. Again, I'm eternally grateful to her for everything she did for our children in my absence. I should have been there for my kids and done more for them, but I wasn't capable of being a good father while I was using drugs. Am I using drugs as a scapegoat? I don't think so. Being a dad just wasn't in me when I was strung out. Some of you may say no matter what my kids needed me, but I maintain they didn't need me while I was using.

I didn't always show my son love, but I always loved him. Since I've been clean I've made ample strides in our relationship. I spend time with Markco when I can, and I often surprise him with a pair of white tennis shoes because he has this thing for them. I could buy Markco an autographed pair of Air Jordans, but if they're not white he won't wear them. As you might expect I have to carefully choose places for our outings. I'll always remember the day I took Markco to Carowinds, an amusement park in Charlotte, N.C. He was really excited and had a ball eating Dippin' Dots! When I'm back in South Carolina I see Markco at his mom's house though he lives in a group home with other autistic adults.

I discussed my daughter jumping in my arms on Christmas Eve 2009. A month prior I'd visited Markco during Thanksgiving. When Markco sees me he always smiles and signs father by placing his thumb against his forehead. Clearly I wasn't always a good father to him, but he was always happy to see me and always knew who I was. On this day Markco signed father and then said daddy. For the first time in my life I heard my son call me daddy. I cried and will never be able to adequately express my feelings in that moment.

Despite how much our relationship has grown, I still have trouble accepting Markco's autism. Does that make me a bad person or a horrible father? I don't think so. It makes me human. Perhaps I think it's somehow my fault. I know a woman who was devastated after miscarrying and through tears asked her doctor whether she'd done anything wrong. She hadn't, but I think when something happens to a child born or unborn a parent's first inclination is to assume blame.

So maybe I feel I'm to blame for Markco's autism and that's why I struggle in my relationship with him. I don't know. I know I'm really trying and that's what counts. I'll continue visiting him, showing him I love him and praying to the God of my understanding for acceptance of his autism.

Listen, I used to get really angry when I overheard someone jokingly call another person retarded. Autism isn't a form of mental retardation, and many autistic people are quite intelligent, but it still pissed me off. I've been able to let that go, and hopefully in time I'll lose the negative emotions I harbor about Markco's autism.

The fact of the matter is I'm crazy about my children and love Markco and Sade more than anything. Markco will always have a very special place in my heart. I just hope and pray he's cognitively able to know that.

Chapter 15

Working At MCVET

Thanks for indulging me while I talked about Markco. Now back to MCVET.

I told you I tried to keep my emotions in check after leaving my job interview at MCVET but really thought I'd nailed it. As you know, I was right.

I was hired as MCVET's intake outreach coordinator, which meant I was responsible for placing men and women at the facility. Simply put, my charge was to fill MCVET's beds with people who needed our services to repair their lives. Filling MCVET's beds wasn't easy. There are thousands of people who need substance abuse treatment or who are homeless, but remember MCVET is exclusive to veterans. Though many veterans needed MCVET, it wasn't always easy to get them to come. Some days I literally walked Baltimore's streets trying to find suitable candidates for MCVET. I also communicated with people at homeless shelters in search of clients.

I took my job seriously and went out of my way to help people. In 2010 a brother from Virginia who'd been accepted at MCVET missed his bus and called me. I told him to catch the next bus and I'd wait. The next bus was 40 minutes late, but I waited even though he arrived two hours past quitting time. I later heard from a few co-workers that the man sang my praises for waiting. I remember how hard it was for me to walk through MCVET's doors on Aug. 22, 2002. I didn't want his first impression of MCVET to be its employees didn't care.

Going to work at MCVET felt great and working in the facility where I got clean was quite humbling. But even after getting the job I was still in for a big surprise...

Remember Mr. Metts and his classes? Well guess who taught a class at MCVET? That's right. Me. The guy who was ashamed to say his name in class taught at MCVET. I'm sure I don't have to tell you I was flooded with memories of Mr. Metts during my first class, which I taught on July 14, 2010. In some respects I felt as though the world had slowed down just a bit that day. As I stood before my students I couldn't help but wonder whether Mr. Metts had felt some of the same emotions that were swirling through me: gratitude, humility and pride. I was grateful MCVET administrators thought I was capable of teaching a class and had some valuable insight to offer. I was humbled to be given a chance to give back to a facility that had given so much to me. And I was proud that just eight years after first sitting in a MCVET classroom as a student I was back there as an instructor.

Before my first class I pondered what information would be useful to the students. The more I thought the clearer it became, and I chose to discuss balance in recovery. Balance plays a huge role in my life. I get up at 5:30 a.m., arrive at work a half hour early, attend an NA meeting almost daily, work out regularly and continuously nurture the personal relationships I've built since getting clean. While discussing those things I carefully explained to my students why I need that structure in my life. The students were receptive to my teaching style and sat on the edge of their seats while I spoke. I'd given numerous speeches at NA meetings during the eleven years since I've been clean, but I'd never experienced anything like my first class.

After it was over the students told me how much they appreciated the information. The feeling I got in those moments can't compare to hearing Markco say daddy, but it's certainly among the best feelings in my life. And for a man who's had as many highs and lows as I have – no pun intended – that's saying something.

Have you ever had an instructor who talked too much or too long? Not me. I allowed my students to participate in class and encouraged them to ask questions and share their thoughts. Things went well with my class, and I looked forward to teaching on Mondays and Wednesdays. Word spread around MCVET about my class, and more students began attending. A few administrators even sat in on my class because they heard good things about it.

My inspiration to teach emanated from the immense gratitude I have for my second chance at life. I wasn't revived by an emergency room doctor at Maryland Shock Trauma or in a coma for two years before miraculously awakening, but you might as well say God gave me a second chance at life when he sent me to MCVET on Aug. 22, 2002.

MCVET is a Godsend for drug addicts and homeless people. To stand in front of a class of MCVET students and give back what was given to me was really mind blowing. To share my experiences, impart wisdom and offer hope to students surpassed my wildest dreams!

Before my first class ended I talked about becoming humble men and women of God and told the students I became a better person when I accepted who I was and others for who they were. I also told the students I've learned no matter what I do God loves me unconditionally and I try to implement unconditional love in my life every day. I don't always succeed but at least I'm making a conscious effort.

Teaching at MCVET felt like a bonus, or extra gravy as the old folk say, and it was inspiring. I wasn't materially rich by any stretch but felt spiritually rich beyond belief. What God did for me was nothing shy of a miracle. When I was strung out on crack I never gave a moment's thought to a rehab facility, much less working in one. I figured I'd get high the rest of my life until drugs and alcohol took my life. Thanks to God I got to work at MCVET and help make a difference in the lives of men and women in whose shoes I once walked. My spiritual journey was strengthened every time I taught at MCVET, and for that I'm truly grateful.

Chapter 16

Reflections Of Change

Look up the word reflection in a dictionary and among the definitions you'll see are "a thought, idea or opinion formed or a remark made as a result of meditation."

Look up change and you'll find "to undergo transformation, transition or substitution."

As I ponder reflection and change, I vividly see the profound existence of them in my life. Reflection isn't easy, particularly soul-searching reflection. There's no question reflection and change have played a significant role in my evolution. Ten years ago I was a drug addict but today I'm in recovery and doing well. When I got high the crack and marijuana I smoked sometimes caused hallucinations, but even in my most drug-induced state I never imagined my life as it is now. Back in the day all I pictured was getting high. I couldn't see the life I have now or fathom a day when I'd routinely speak at NA meetings. Back then I couldn't dream of going a day without drugs or alcohol.

The transformation in my life has been fantastic, and with each passing moment I'm changing into the man I truly believe God intended. Sure I still make mistakes and come up short, but now I realize I don't need drugs or alcohol to cope with my mistakes and shortcomings.

Carl Lewis is one of the most famous track and field athletes of all time and was once voted "Olympian of the Century" by *Sports Illustrated*. I'm no Carl Lewis, but back in the day I was called a runner because when faced with fear or something unpleasant I ran away.

Today I'm not a runner and face life head on. I deal with my problems like a man and without drugs and alcohol to guide me.

I've lost my mother, father and three siblings. My marriage didn't last, my son is autistic and sometimes my daughter still has ill feelings over my former life. I screwed up some pretty good jobs in my day, and I've endured much heartache in the love department. Through all of my pain and disappointment I've grown emotionally and mentally, learned to trust God and learned to believe in my ability to make good decisions and do the next right thing.

At times I've wondered why my life turned out the way it did, but as I've grown emotionally, mentally and spiritually I've realized the real question is who am I to be excluded from life's ups and downs?

And believe it or not, if I had a choice to rewind the clock I probably wouldn't because I realize the heartbreak, disappointment, failure and success I've experienced helped mold me into the man I am today.

Instead of awakening with thoughts of getting high, I awaken thanking God for my clear mind. Instead of wasting my money on drugs and alcohol I wisely invest it. I have countless reasons to be grateful for things I foolishly took for granted years ago, and I awaken each morning with thanksgiving in my heart. You see, all I have to do is look at the hideous photo I keep in my wallet and remember that strung out man who when soaking wet barely weighted a buck fifty. I simply have to remember his broken spirit, messed-up mind and pitiful life before I start thinking about the way God has blessed me.

Today the purpose of my life is helping others turn around their lives by being of service to them and providing them with hope. Legendary college basketball coach John Wooden said it's what you learn after you know it all that counts. For years I thought I had it all figured out but now I understand what really counts is what I've

learned since getting clean and learning to trust in God.

Chapter 17

One Day At A Time

During my three-month evaluation at MCVET I was given an overall ranking of majority excellent, meaning my supervisors were highly pleased with my work performance. In fact, I began spending one Saturday a month at MCVET for intake to provide an extra day for potential clients to enroll. It meant working on the weekend but was a small price to pay for the chance to help save someone's life. I'll always remember the jubilation I felt when I enrolled my first Saturday client after a month of working weekends. I was a little disappointed it took so long but had to accept that things happen on God's time.

Things continued going well at work, and I was enjoying a close relationship with Sade while becoming more accepting of Markco's autism. As you'll recall from an earlier chapter things with Sade weren't always good. To be honest our relationship was pretty non-existent for many years, and while I don't think she hated me I know I wasn't among her favorite people for obvious and understandable reasons. Yet thanks to her having the courage to email me one day we're back in each other's lives. Our relationship isn't perfect but is a trillion times better than it was. And even though I have my sponsor, my sponsees and many close friends, some days Sade is my biggest support system. I can't tell you how beautiful it is to have a relationship with the daughter I feared I'd lost forever. Knowing Sade loves me and having her in my life mean more to mean than just about anything.

To continue with my good news, I easily re-adjusted to being back in Baltimore and got involved with a pretty active home group. I also started spending time with some of the cats I got clean with, including Terry C. and Dotson C., and I pretty much furnished my apartment rather inexpensively through Craigslist.

Yet despite all of that, I can't get ahead of myself and start taking things for granted. And I most certainly can't ever assume I've got this. You see even if I live to be ninety-five, I will always be a recovering addict and must take things one day at a time. Does one day at a time mean I live only in the present? Does it mean I never plan for the future? Of course not. Everyone including recovering addicts must plan ahead. I have to keep a budget, go grocery shopping, schedule doctor's appointments and try to book flights and hotel rooms in advance to save money. One day at a time has a profound meaning for recovering addicts. In short, it's a much-needed reality check.

As a recovering addict I can't get cocky and assume because I've been clean for eleven years I've got recovery licked. I can't stop communicating with Don and my sponsees and attending NA meetings. And I sure as hell can't convince myself one itty bitty little shot won't hurt me. Talking to Don helps keep me grounded, especially when I feel some of my bad habits trying to reemerge. Being there for my sponsees reassures them and reminds me people look to me for guidance, support and wisdom. Not succumbing to the urge to down one itty bitty little shot keeps me from reverting to the dreadful life I lived before Aug. 22, 2002, because as we say at the end of meetings one drink is too many and a thousand aren't enough. The minute I drink a shot I'll also foolishly persuade myself I can handle smoking just a little crack…

So how do I take things one day at a time? With God's help I've learned to accept my powerlessness. I did it my way for more than twenty years before accepting on Aug. 22, 2002, that my way wasn't working. Frank Sinatra's hit "My Way" made him a ton of dough, but all my way brought me were misery, emptiness, heartache and pain. In chapter eight I discussed how hard it is to change, but by allowing God to take control of my life I'm learning how to accept my powerlessness and surrender to Him. I'm realizing what it means to do the possible and let God do the impossible. I'm embracing my humanness and accepting that at times I'm going to falter. I'm still a work in progress, but by surrendering to God I more easily accept who I am and my limitations. Through internal and aggressive self-acceptance I've found the innermost part of me, a part I ignored for a very long time. I used to live with pain, ill will, failure and disappointment every day, and every day I tried to bury the pain, ill will, failure and disappointment with cocaine, booze and women. With God's help the pain, ill will, failure and disappointment have been replaced with acceptance, hope, faith and trust and, most importantly, with a genuine love of purpose for my life.

Today as I enjoy a life I couldn't possibly have conceived of ten years ago, I realize I must continue, with God's help, traveling the road leading to the real Michael Lee Strong. If I don't I could relapse and return to the phony Michael who abused his body with cocaine, booze and women for more than twenty years. I want no part of that pseudo Michael but instead want to continue trying to become the man God intended. Today I wouldn't dream of going two weeks without communicating with Sade, much less years as I once did. Today I'm appreciative for any job with which I'm blessed and give 100 percent every day. I'm more patient, more tolerant, more humble and more forgiving. I keep in touch with my siblings and tell people I love them rather than assume they know. Today I don't try to mask my feelings or run from them; I confront them head on and deal with them. I don't turn to cocaine, booze and women to solve my problems but accept they were a huge source of my problems in the first place. By practicing one day at a time I'm slowly but surely becoming the man God intended. And instead of always seeking the next best thing – just as addicts always seek their next high – I'm truly grateful for where I am right now in this very moment. I'm comfortable in my own skin these days because I know I'm doing what God commands and being of service to others. It's no longer all about me, and boy does that feel good!

By practicing one day at a time I inch closer to my spiritual center where I find innermost peace. I talk to God every day and make no apologies for that. The time I spend alone with Him is precious. Having a one-on-one conversation with God as I walk in a park or drive down a country road helps me get closer to Him because He lives in my heart. Back in the day I searched the world looking for peace and never found it. I didn't find it in Guam, my favorite place on Earth, or in Germany where I met Silvia. Once I let go and let God I found peace within. Just like happiness, peace starts within. If you're not happy no one can make you happy. Likewise, no one can give you peace. Since I've established a close relationship with God my purpose has become more transparent and I've begun practicing unconditional love.

I'm so grateful I'm able to resist the urge to smoke crack, take a drink or have sex with a woman just because she's attractive and willing. I'm so grateful I'm a much better person than I was eleven years ago, five years ago or even one year ago. I'm grateful I can apply one day at a time to my life in meaningful ways. I'm grateful for my family, my friends, my brothers and sisters in the struggle and my job at MCVET. I'm grateful I could be brutally honest in this book about my failures and successes, ups and downs and highs and lows. And I'm grateful for God's presence in my life and the way He's helping me become the man He intended.

Chapter 18

Sex and Relationships

Every day I'm becoming the man I think God intended, but I haven't forgotten about the person I used to be.

When I think about sex and relationships my mind goes in for a tailspin. And when I think about the role sex and relationships have played in my life, I think about women I dated back in the day and how sex was basically all we had going for us – at least from my perspective. I think about how important sex was to me and how it didn't matter whether I really knew the women well or liked them. To me the important thing was the sex, and if they were willing so was I. I've had sex with black women, white women, Hispanic women, Asian women and African women. You name it. I've done it. And given my travels during eight years in the Air Force, I've had sex with women all over the world – literally.

Drugs remove sexual inhibitions. There are plenty of sexual acts I wouldn't dare perform now that I readily did while high. Some of you reading this may think I had it going on, but when I reflect on the worthless and useless sex-only relationships I had it makes me sick and ashamed. That behavior is in stark contrast to the way I view sex and relationships today. I realize now I was using sex to try to solve my internal problems. I was attacking a spiritual problem with a physical solution and it didn't work. I was so lost spiritually that I repeatedly tried to make myself feel better with sex. Instead of taking a long, hard look at myself and assessing what was wrong, I tried masking my problems in bed. It was nothing for me to meet a woman, take her out for dinner or a movie and have sex with her before the night was over. I was having unprotected sex with women I barely knew, foolishly playing Russian roulette with my life. Fortunately God protected me.

Many of my sexual escapades involved drug use, but most were an attempt to fill the spiritual void in my life. I just wasn't sure who I was from a spiritual standpoint, and while running around having sex here, there and everywhere I became nearly as addicted to it as I was to drugs. I said nearly because I'm not addicted to sex. In fact, the opposite is true about me. Nowadays I can be content in a monogamous relationship where sex is hardly the focal point or I can be content without sex period. I practice celibacy without experiencing sleepless nights or having to take cold showers. How can I do that? As I've gotten clean and gotten closer to God, I've gotten to know and love me. I've taken time to get inside Michael's head and explore my likes and dislikes. Now don't get it twisted. I still enjoy sex, but it's no longer something I have to have, something that drives me or the biggest part of my relationships. I now fully understand sex is something beautiful to be shared between two people who love each other or have decided to give themselves to each other. I was way grown before I really got that, but instead of being ashamed I'm celebrating because I got it. There's no harm in not knowing something; after all we can't all be Einstein. The harm comes when you don't know and don't try to learn.

I said I used to have sex with all types of women and that's true. I also said I didn't always use protection. What I haven't told you is that some of my former sexual encounters were downright dangerous. Let me explain.

Once I had some drugs and happened upon a couple desperately looking to cop. So being the low-down person I was at the time, I told the man I'd share my drugs with them if he found me a woman with whom to have sex. Believe it or not he offered his wife. Your eyes aren't playing tricks on you. The man offered his own wife. So there I was in some crack house having unprotected sex with this man's wife while he got high and watched. I was certainly no saint in this situation. I was committing adultery and being despicable, but I can't imagine how the man felt once the drugs wore off and he realized he'd offered his wife to a stranger for drugs. When it was all said and done I'm sure the brother felt really bad. Hell, for all I know the incident caused some problems in their marriage later on. But back to me. No question my actions were repulsive and stupid. The man could have come to his senses during the actual sexual act and kicked my ass or killed me. Or he could have come after me days, weeks or months later and done me in. The brother never came after me, but my behavior was certainly dangerous to say the least.

I've thought about that night over the years and I'm grateful the guy didn't come after me. On the one hand he offered his wife in exchange for drugs, and I gave them some drugs. But on the other hand what I did was pretty bad. When that night crosses my mind what I mainly think about is how insane I was and just how far down the moral chain I'd spiraled.

Another former sexual escapade for which I feel shame is the time I was with two sisters. Here again, it was all about the basic principle of supply and demand. The sisters wanted drugs, and I was more than happy to provide drugs for sex. During my really grimy days I also had sex with lesbians because, again, they wanted the drugs I possessed and I wanted sex. Suffice it to say I was out of control and drew a line only at men.

During this sex-crazed time in my life having sex with many women became my norm. I've heard some say having casual sex or being promiscuous is a sign of low self-esteem. I concur. Why would anyone want to have sex with more than one person at a time? Some of you may think the drugs I ingested really fried my brain and I don't know what I'm missing. Trust me. I know and I don't miss it. When I think about my former sexual encounters I feel dirty, low and empty. What I know now is things were so bad back then 'til even the drugs weren't enough to fill the void existing in me. It was so deep instead of realizing I needed help I continued disrespecting women and myself. I get really bummed when I think of what my mother would have thought about my treatment of women. I know she would have loved me despite it, but my actions would have broken her heart.

Listen, I know I'm not the only brother to sleep with sisters simultaneously. Hell, many cats have done that without drugs. I also know straight men have sex with lesbians. But again, I can speak only for Michael. The Michael of today would never think about doing that or being with two women at the same time. When I think about those sisters, the lesbians with whom I had sex and that man's wife I feel bad. But I've had to forgive myself for the way I used to mistreat women and myself.

Men get a lot of misinformation about sex. I spoke on this in a previous chapter but it's so dear to me it's worth repeating. A lot of men are encouraged to have as many sexual experiences as they can. I guess we think having multiple sexual partners will make us better lovers, but there's so much more to being a good lover than having sex. Hell, that's the easy part. Truly loving someone involves more than the physical act. I obviously bought into the misinformation and the hype and got caught up in trying to have as many notches in my sexual belt as possible. I was lured into a type of menticide, or a systematic and intentional undermining of a person's conscious mind. A simpler way to explain it is if someone tells you something often enough you start believing it. In today's lingo you start drinking the Kool-Aid. Think about it. A little black kid from the ghetto has above-average intelligence but constantly hears his teachers say poor, black kids aren't smart. While it's true that little black kid is smart, chances are he'll start performing poorly on tests, papers and homework assignments because his teachers' words get in his head. People used to call me a ladies' man and a player. I knew I wasn't and wanted to be that faithful brother who took care of his woman and loved only her. I wanted to be that brother who was telling the truth when he called to say he was working late. Romans 7:9 says: For the good which I will, I do not; but the evil which I will not, that I do. When I was married I wanted to be a good, faithful husband to LaDonna; however, I felt compelled to be something I wasn't. I can't say unequivocally whether it was peer pressure or menticide. I just know between my lack of sexual inhibitions spawned by the drugs and buying into what others said I was, I became the epitome of a sorry ass brother. Sex became almost as important to me as getting high, and I hurt a lot of women in the process. Especially painful is knowing I ruined what could have been a very good marriage with a woman who really loved me, not to mention I forced my children to live in a broken home. We talk a lot about forgiveness in Narcotics Anonymous. I'm still forgiving myself for behaving so contrary to the man I was.

Today I see women from the neck up and no longer see them as sex objects. Today I look for the soul of a woman. There's also a big difference today in how I see me. I'm not trying to be perfect, but I'm striving for improvement. I can be happy when I'm not in a relationship and when I'm not sexually active. In fact, I've been abstinent for more than three years. I'm abstinent because I have a deep-rooted respect for myself that was missing before. I'm finally the person I wanted to be all along, and I get to know women from the inside out. Today I'm not pressured into relationships – or sexual encounters – because of what somebody else thinks I should do. Today I'm my own man and I'm striving to do what Shakespeare said: To thine own self be true. Today I'm trying to be obedient to the God of my understanding.

Chapter 19

Sade

I spent a chapter on my son. Now it's time to kick it about my daughter.

When I was younger I heard men talk about the special bond they had with their daughters, and I often heard women discuss how girls had their fathers wrapped around their fingers. But it's one thing to hear something and another thing to experience it. That rang true when Lynnethia Sade Strong was born at 5:15 a.m. on Friday, June 26, 1987. Sade, the younger of my two children, was born at the Naval Hospital in Agana, Guam, while I was in the Air Force. Sade was named after her mother's sister, Lynnethia, and my favorite singer, Sade. Since she was a baby we've called her Sade.

As much as I love my son, the truth is I wasn't sure I wanted more children. Markco, as you'll recall, is autistic and went through so much when he was just a baby. After having one autistic child I was fearful any additional children would also have autism or some other disorder, and I wasn't sure I could handle that. But LaDonna and I talked after she found out she was pregnant, and we decided to go forward with the pregnancy. Even though I didn't realize it at the time, by not asking LaDonna to terminate the pregnancy I was letting go and letting God.

I had learned a lot from Markco's birth and LaDonna had, too. Once I let go of my fear about Sade being born with something wrong, I warmed up to the idea of being a dad again and having a playmate for Markco. I had gone with LaDonna to Lamaze classes when she was pregnant with Markco and had no problem going again. I'm a stickler for being prepared and believe in being early. Needless to say, LaDonna's suitcase was packed, by the door and ready to go. We also had Pampers, Similac and other necessary items stockpiled.

I'm not sure exactly what time LaDonna awakened me on June 24, but if memory serves me correctly it was between 10 p.m. and 11 p.m. She told me she was in labor so I jumped up and sprang into action. You know, at that time in the marriage I was actually a pretty good husband. I'd had some indiscretions as I've disclosed, but when LaDonna was pregnant with Sade I wasn't so bad. But back to

Sade.

She was a beautiful baby with a head full of curly hair just like her mom. I know all men say their baby girls are beautiful but Sade really was! She was a happy baby and instantly captured my heart. I was in the delivery room crying happy tears when she was born and even cut the umbilical cord. Markco, Sade and I spent practically every day at the beach while living in Guam, and I spent a lot of quality time with them. Suffice it to say we were inseparable. I've told many people Guam is my favorite place on earth and if I learned I had only a month to live I'd spend some of my last days there. I love Guam because of its climate and because Sade was born there. I also have great memories of spending so much time with my children there. When I think about how happy Sade, Markco and I were while spending hours on the beach, it's hard to understand how I allowed drugs and alcohol to practically destroy our relationship. But let me not digress.

As best LaDonna and I could tell – and from all indications from the doctors – Sade was a healthy baby. And it didn't take long for us to realize she was smart. She was walking at eight months, and at eighteen months she could get up at night and go to the bathroom by herself. By two and a half she was already tying her shoes! Sade was always full of energy and conversation. In fact, one of my most cherished memories of her is accompanying her on her first day of school. It's hard to express just how special that was, and I could hardly believe my baby girl was all grown up. Sade was happy about school and fit right in with her classmates. When she got home that day she excitedly told her mother and me all about her very first day of school.

I have extremely fond memories of taking Sade to school on her first day, but I don't have an abundance of memories from her early years. I wasn't there when she first tried out for organized sports or when she acted in her first school play. I didn't attend her assemblies and grin like a proud papa when she received awards or recognition. But there's more. I wasn't around to answer her questions when my baby girl started liking boys or to help her deal with the inevitable frustration that emerges during that period in a teenage girl's life. I wasn't there when Sade first experienced heartbreak, and I didn't see my baby all dressed up and looking beautiful for her high school prom.

I should have been there for many of those momentous events in Sade's life. After LaDonna and I split for good I bounced from state to state and couldn't attend every important function in Sade's life, but despite the divorce I could have and should have done much better by her and Markco. I sometimes cry when I think about the important, once-in-a-lifetime events I missed. It hurts when I think about not being there for my baby girl when she needed me. I feel really bad and ashamed and don't need anyone to tell me I let Sade down. I also cry because I'm aware of the ways in which my absence could have influenced her. I can't tell you how many times I've heard women who grew up without their fathers acknowledge looking for love in all the wrong places. Many of you probably know a woman who became promiscuous while searching for the love she didn't get from her father. And some of you may know a woman who married a much older man, the father figure she never had. Had Sade fallen into either of those traps, I would have been chiefly to blame. Fortunately she didn't.

I never intended to become a drug addict, but I did and I can't change that. I also can't get back the precious time I missed with Sade or undo the hurt and pain I caused her. Lord knows I would if I could. What I can do moving forward is continue being the best father I can to her. She's grown with a son of her own now, but she's still my daughter and will always be my baby girl. She needs me in her life and so does her son, Amari. Whenever I can I spend time with that adorable little boy, who warms my soul when he calls me PaPa Strong.

"You've come a long way, baby" was a slogan made popular decades ago by Virginia Slims cigarettes. My relationship with Sade has come a long way, but we still have a way to go and I don't take it for granted. There was a time when Sade's feelings for me vacillated between anger and bitterness, but that's not the case today. Our relationship isn't perfect but is much better than it used to be and for that I'm eternally grateful. I'm very proud of the young woman Sade has become. She's relentless when she really wants something, and she knows how to persevere. Despite being a single mom she managed to finish college, which made me incredibly happy. She has a college degree and played the hand life dealt her without making excuses or turning to drugs and alcohol. Sade wouldn't have grown into the determined young woman she is without her mother, LaDonna Comera Roberts Strong, who was mother and father to her and her brother. LaDonna was in Sade's corner when drugs and alcohol kept me out. Even though we divorced more than twenty years ago, I will always be indebted to her for the way she raised our children.

I melt when I hear Sade lovingly refer to me as her daddy. I'm overwhelmed with joy because I know the pendulum could easily have swung the other way. In May 2012 I traveled to North Carolina to celebrate four years of clean time with one of my sponsees. A dynamic, no-holds-barred sister spoke at his celebration and kept it real. But even this tough sister with double-digit clean time broke down while talking about the son who can't forgive her for the years she missed in his life. She cried while saying he wants nothing to do with her, and it's not lost on me Sade could feel the same way about me. Thankfully Sade has allowed me to reenter her life and also be part of her son's life. I know that's a blessing. To be clear, our relationship hasn't always been easy. Remember I'm the guy who year in and year out missed birthdays, broke promises and didn't give his kids anything for Christmas. I wanted to attend their birthday parties and send or hand deliver Christmas presents, and I wanted to be there when they were sick and when Sade went on her first date. I wanted to do all of that but did very little of it. I've forgiven myself though honestly I sometimes question whether I'm worthy of their love.

Fortunately my children have decided I am worthy of their love and give it freely. When Sade and I started rekindling our relationship it was tough because we didn't know each other. I wanted to become daddy all over again, but by the time we reunited Sade was older and instead of a daddy needed a father. Trust me when I say she let me know that, too. Sade isn't short on words, and she's very emotional. If I make her cry she doesn't go easy on me – and she shouldn't. I never intentionally upset her, but I strive not to overcompensate for the missed years by letting her get away with murder. If she does something wrong or is headed down a bad path I tell her. Despite all that has transpired between us and everything I missed, Sade and I are developing a really beautiful relationship. She even calls me for guidance before making a potentially life-changing decision. Imagine that. A young woman who back in the day couldn't count on me for much of anything now calls me for advice. Suffice it to say God has shown me favor when it comes to my daughter and my son. Sade and I have come a long way since she used to call me Mike, as though I was the guy next door or a clerk at a nearby convenience store. Today she wouldn't dare call me Mike, and her face brightens when she sees me. Between Facebook, text messages and phone calls, Sade and I are in pretty constant communication. I drive to South Carolina several times a year to see her, Amari and Markco, and one of these days I'm going to arrange for Sade and Amari to visit me in Maryland. I can just picture the three of us strolling around The Inner Harbor as Amari marvels at the sights and sounds. I love Sade with all of my heart and soul and pray our relationship keeps getting stronger.

Chapter 20

Wreckage From the Past

Now that I've discussed my relationship with my daughter, let me get back into the thick of things.

Some days are just better than others and you awaken feeling great after a good night's sleep. You're in a great mood, at peace and ready for a productive day at the office. I smile just thinking about those kinds of days. But some days you awaken after a restless night. You've got a lot on your mind, you're tired and you don't feel like going to work. Yep. Some days are just better than others.

In late January 2012 I had a day I'll always remember; though it's certainly a day I'd love to forget. It began like most days. I awoke around 5:30, made my bed, had a few cups of coffee and spent some time talking to God before showering and leaving for work. After getting off work I drove north on Interstate Ninety-five to Harford County, where I work part-time at a homeless shelter. Work at the shelter was fine, and I had no clue about what I was going to encounter when I got off. Sometimes we have an intuition about things, but believe me you I had no idea what was headed my way. I left the shelter at midnight like always and proceeded down the interstate back to Baltimore. My plan was to go home, crash and get up for work the next day. It was a beautiful winter night, the moon and stars shone brightly, Yancyy was wailing in my ears and I was in a good mood.

So there I was headed home when I noticed a police car behind me. I wasn't pressed because I wasn't speeding, my insurance and registration were current and I possessed a valid driver's license. Some drivers get nervous when a police car is behind them, but I knew everything was in order so I kept driving, jamming to Yancyy and thinking about how nice my bed was going to feel. The officer stayed behind me for a while before dropping off to the left, slowing down to a crawl and turning on his lights. Then he got back behind me and turned on the siren, so I immediately pulled over and wondered what the hell was going on. I drive the speed limit and haven't had a ticket in 24 years. I don't dart in and out of lanes, and when I see a flashing sign warning the lane I'm in will close I get over instead of pushing the envelope and waiting until the last possible second before the lane runs out. By the way, I was driving a non-descript Nissan Sentra – hardly a car to arouse suspicion – and I couldn't figure out why I was being pulled. Nonetheless, I knew exactly what to do. I pulled over, got my driver's license out of my wallet and reached for my registration and proof of insurance.

The officer approached on the passenger's side and said hello. I spoke and asked him how I could help him while still wondering why in the hell I'd been pulled. The white officer seemed at ease though it was dark outside and we were in one of the country's most dangerous cities. I was donned in neatly pressed black slacks and a blue shirt with a matching tie, and I was sporting a fresh haircut. My shoes were spit-shined – a carryover from my Air Force days – though the officer couldn't see that in the dark. After I asked how I could help, he told me I had an expired emissions test. Whew! Even though I'd been back in Maryland eighteen months at this point, I'd forgotten the state is big on emissions tests. I told the officer that and he said it was okay. He also said he'd let me go with only a warning, though he asked for my license to run a background check. I knew I hadn't had any run-ins with the law since I was arrested ten years prior for theft, so as he walked back to his squad car I sat in my ride relieved to be getting only a warning. A warning meant I wouldn't have to cough up any dough or go to court. As I sat I, kept thinking it shouldn't take him long to write the warning ticket and in minutes I'd be back on the highway headed home. Not exactly. A few minutes went by, then a few more and then a few more. The longer I sat, the more uneasy I felt, and it didn't take rocket science to know something was amiss. A second siren interrupted my thoughts, and in less than a minute the officer who pulled me and the one who'd just arrived were both walking toward my car and ordering me to step out of my vehicle. Now thoughts were swirling through my mind. I didn't know what to think or what to expect. Here I was a lone black man on a Baltimore highway being ordered out of my vehicle by two white officers. I won't exaggerate and say Rodney King crossed my mind, but I was quite concerned at this point. I was telling the truth earlier when I said I wasn't pressed at first, but now I was more than pressed. You don't live five decades without learning the proper way to get out of a vehicle when ordered by police, so I got out very slowly. One of the officers told me there was a ten-year-old warrant for my arrest and ordered me to put my hands behind my back. I immediately complied. Again, I was by myself with two white police officers so I did exactly as they instructed while praying neither of them tried any bullshit. I didn't know what to expect moving forward, but I certainly didn't want to do or say anything either of them could misconstrue as threatening. It was painfully clear by now my night wasn't going to go as planned, but at least I wanted to avoid ending up on the wrong side of a knuckle sandwich or a nightstick.

As I was putting my hands behind my back I calmly told the officers I had abated the charge for which the warrant had been issued. One of them quickly replied that might be the case but because of what came up on the license check they were still obligated to take me to central booking. Hearing the words central booking sent fear and shivers down my spine. I don't know how much you know about Baltimore, but suffice it to say the city is infamous for its homicide rate. For ten consecutive years back in the nineties, the city had three hundred or more murders per year. One year during that stretch three hundred and fifty-eight people were killed – nearly a person a day. I'm no wuss, but the thought of going to central booking where I might get stuck in a cell with some cat in for murder was hardly appealing. When I hung out with the lowest of the low in Baltimore I heard a lot of stories about central booking.

Every story I heard was bad. And remember that though I was charged in 2002 with stealing computers from the city, the arresting officer didn't handcuff me but instead let me discreetly gather my things and leave the office. Imagine how I felt being handcuffed for the first time at age fifty. I was placed in the police cruiser headed for the dreaded central booking. As soon as we pulled off for the short ride downtown I had a quick jam session with God. I told Him I didn't know what to do and asked Him to please guide me. The officer and I made small talk and he promised not to have my car towed as long as I took care of the warrant and got released. That was cool with me because I wanted nothing more than to get downtown, clear up the matter and get the hell of out central booking ASAP.

So far no harm had come to me, the officers had been nice and it looked as though soon this would all be just a memory. But even so, for a brother in recovery the rubber was meeting the road. I mean here I was approaching ten years of clean time and I had a really good full-time job and a not-too-shabby part-time gig. I had a car and my own place, and I was in relatively good physical condition and doing well spiritually. Yet despite all of that, I was in the back of

a police cruiser on my way to central booking at one o'clock in the

morning. I wondered why God was allowing this to happen to me

until I realized the situation in which I found myself involved human

error. At one point I'd broken the law by stealing computers from my

employer. I knew I'd already taken care of the court-ordered

restitution but systems aren't fail proof and glitches happen. So I

started telling myself, *Mike, just get through this and get back to your life.*

Just get through this and get back to your life.

Outside central booking was a line of men in handcuffs waiting

to be processed. They were mostly young black males with a

sprinkling of white and Hispanic men. When I finally got inside I was

shocked and sickened by what I saw. I was taken into a room for a

strip search and then placed in a concrete holding cell built for four

but housing eight. Some of the cells were built for ten but had

twenty-five to thirty people crammed inside, so I guess I got off easy.

I know when you get arrested it's not like you're going to be housed

inside posh quarters with all-you-can-eat hors d'oeuvres, but what

happened to innocent until proven guilty? In central booking people

are treated like animals, regardless of the offense with which they're charged or regardless of their guilt or innocence. What I truly couldn't understand was why on earth anyone would willingly do anything that could land him or her in such an un-Godly place. I say that because we all know there's a high recidivism rate. If you ask me, anyone who thinks it's okay to endure this type of treatment more than once needs his or her head examined. After being in central booking for just a few minutes I desperately yearned to go home to my small, one-bedroom apartment, take a hot, relaxing shower, lie on my couch and watch TV. But the shower, couch and TV would have to wait. I got to central booking around 1:20 a.m. Friday – when I should have been at home getting my sleep on for work – and didn't leave until 10:45 a.m. Saturday. That's right. I was there for nearly thirty-six hours. A lot happened during that time; fortunately none of it was violent. Thanks to the God of my understanding and the work I do regularly through the 12 Step program, I was able to dig deep, tap into my spirit and get through the ordeal without going crazy. But I won't lie. There was a period during my incarceration when I felt like I was going to lose it. Thankfully and prayerfully I didn't. Before Aug. 22, 2002, there's no way I would have been able to get through that nightmare as gracefully as I did. Brothers, let me drop some

science on you. Don't get stuck in the system and become

accustomed to being treated like animals. We are kings. We're not

court jesters, pack mules, field niggas, physical abusers or genocidal

or homicidal maniacs. Learn who you are, not what you think you are

or what someone else thinks you are. Stop feeding into destructive

thoughts and behaviors, actions that can destroy you, your families

and your communities. And learn to turn negatives into positives.

Since becoming clean I've tried to turn negatives into positives,

and I've certainly done it since my central booking ordeal. I could

whine about how it sucked to get arrested and taken to central

booking, a smelly, filthy place. I could bitch about having to pay

more than three hundred dollars to clear the warrant, though I had

paid all of the required money years ago. (Incidentally the matter was

cleared up four months later and I got reimbursed.) Instead of

whining and bitching, I've vowed to never do anything that could

land me within five miles of central booking. I also thank God for

protecting me that night from the cops and the guys with whom I

was detained. I know all cops aren't bad, but I also know all cops

aren't good. Thank God those two arresting officers weren't some racist rednecks who hide behind a badge because had they been Lord only knows what shape I would have been in when I arrived at central booking – if I arrived. And once inside anything could have gone haywire. For example, some of the cats could have tried to jump me. Fortunately as I said nothing violent went down. I even managed to get some sleep though be damn clear I slept with one eye open and was all too ready to leave central booking when Larry P. came to spring me. I've shared my ordeal at NA meetings and with a few young wannabe brothers in hopes of scaring them onto the straight and narrow path. I will continue thanking God for getting me through it.

Chapter 21

Self Destruction?

I often question why African-Americans are on a self-destructive path, particularly African-American men. It's a valid question given the shape of black America, and certainly a valid question coming from a man who squandered two decades of his life with drugs, alcohol and women. The question needs to be answered, and while I'm no great philosopher I like delving into issues and posing food for thought. Two years ago I started an online think tank comprised of close friends and relatives who kick it back and forth about some of the pressing issues of the day. Topics including politics, religion, education and sports and subjects directly affecting African-Americans often get discussed. We don't always agree, and sometimes people's feelings get a tad bruised, but I'm grateful we have the group because it allows us to dialogue and me to bounce my views on certain subjects off people whose opinions I revere.

I've heard many black people say they've been dealt a bad hand or the system is designed for us to fail. One day several years ago while watching the old "Self-Destruction" video featuring a number of rappers; I really started thinking about this issue. You know what's so interesting? Rap music from back in the day – before lyrics became misogynistic and violent – was very prophetic.

"Self-Destruction" was a helluva song in which the rappers tried to get black folk to wake up, just as Dap, portrayed by actor Laurence Fishburne, tried to do in Spike Lee's hit film "School Daze."

The lyrics in "Self-Destruction" are mind blowing. "Well, today's topic, self-destruction, it really ain't the rap audience that's buggin. It's one or two suckas, ignorant brothers trying to rob and steal from one another." And that's just the beginning. The song goes on: "Pop, pop, pop when it's shot who's to blame? Headlines, front page and rap's the name. MC Delight here to state the bottom line, that black-on-black crime was way before our time."

"Self-Destruction" wasn't the only song that warned us. In "The Message" we heard "Don't push me cause I'm close to the edge. I'm trying not to lose my head. It's like a jungle sometimes it makes me wonder how I keep from going under." And "We're all in the Same Gang" had among its lyrics: "It's straight up madness everywhere I look. Used to be a straight-A student now he's a crook. Robbing people just to smoke or shoot up. Used to have a crew cut, now he's a pooh-put."

Those songs tried to warn us, but unfortunately many of us including yours truly didn't take heed. Hell, I used to throw down at the club when those songs came on, dancing to the very songs preaching about my destructive lifestyle. The good news is I woke up, got my butt in treatment and now thanks to the 12 Step program, the God of my understanding and my own will and determination I'm far removed from that lifestyle. The bad news is millions and millions of black folk are still caught up. Millions of black folk are strung out on drugs, alcohol or both, and far too many of us are involved in black-on-black crime. We're gunning each other down in the streets like dogs over bullshit.

Black folk love to talk about our music, its origins and how much it means to us. And we've all heard someone mention a song that speaks to us. I can name dozens of songs that are meaningful to me. "We Are Family" by Sister Sledge makes me think fondly about my 10 sisters. "A Song for Mama" by Boyz II Men instantly floods my heart with precious memories of Louise Grace Strong. The incomparable Stevie Wonder wrote "Isn't she lovely" to celebrate the birth of his daughter Aisha, but of course that classic makes me think of Sade. And in "All about Love" Maurice White says "I'm trying to tell you, you gotta love you. You gotta love all the beautiful things around you, the trees, the birds. And if there ain't no beauty you gotta make some beauty have mercy listen to me, y'all." Whether you're talking R&B, gospel, reggae, jazz, hip-hop, country or Salsa, music speaks to all of us. I just wish the rap lyrics from back in the day and from some of today's most popular hits would start resonating with black folk, particularly brothers.

A few questions for you to ponder:

- Why is it that more than eighty percent of the violent crimes perpetrated against black males are committed by black males?
- Why are more than seventy-two percent of black children being raised in a single-parent household?

• Why have more than fifty-five percent of black women never been married?

I once read a study labeling incarceration as the primary reason women raise children as single parents. I was never incarcerated when my children were growing up, but I was pretty much an absentee dad just the same. Actually, now that I think about it I was locked up, only my bars weren't metal and I was free to come and go as I pleased. I was locked up inside an insidious world of drugs, alcohol and women. But just what happens when we disappear from our children's lives? What happens to our children when we become so obsessed with money and sex we lose sight of what's most important? What happens to our children when we choose to have unprotected sex and keep making babies in this neighborhood and that neighborhood, knowing full well we aren't properly taking care of the children we already have? Hello? Is anybody home? Is your elevator going all the way to the top? Brothers, we've got to learn to love and be responsible for ourselves. We've got to learn to be responsible for our children and to our children's mothers. The relationship changes when you're no longer with your children's mother or mothers. You don't necessarily have to be responsible for them, but you should still be responsible to them.

That day I was chillin and listening to old school rap I thought about the general tone of rap music back in the day. It wasn't about bitches and ho's and trashing the police. Rap back in the day wasn't all about anger, sex, degradation, violence and greed, as much of it is today. Back then it was feel good music with lyrics rife with knowledge and power. And let's face it; rap from back in the day was just plain bad. "Summertime" by DJ Jazzy Jeff and the Fresh Prince, and "Christmas Rappin'" by Kurtis Blow. Need I say more? When I hear those two songs I start jamming, smiling and reminiscing about the good 'ole days. My question is from where did this damned near insatiable appetite for destructive, misogynistic music come? Why do so many black folk find appealing the lyrics to some of the most destructive music on earth? Why is it when you're sitting at a traffic light and the teenagers in the car next to you have their radio blasting they're often playing music with degrading lyrics but most of those same teenagers can't name all seven continents, the three branches of government or tell you what the first amendment guarantees? Black folk often complain about mistreatment by white folk, but we need to wake up to the egregious way we treat each other. Brothers, look at how you're treating the sisters. And sisters, some of you need to check out how you're treating the brothers. Adults, we must start setting better examples for children – and not just the ones in our bloodlines.

Let's take a trip down memory lane. Remember the attitudes and language that began appearing in gangsta rap videos of the late eighties and early nineties? Can we honestly distance ourselves from the mostly negative impact that music had on the generation that followed? I don't think so, and I'll be the first to assume some of the blame because like many in my generation I turned to the very drugs rapped about in those songs and became an absentee father. Brothers, when we weren't there we created a void in our households that our impressionable sons and daughters tried filling with greed, self-hate, self-obsession and self-destruction. When you think about it, can we even question why some of our children are the way they are? It's almost as though black folk have systematically made a conscious decision to self-destruct. I know not all black folk are self-destructing, so don't jump down my throat and say I'm unfairly lumping all black people into one sorry ass pile. I'm well aware many black folk are maintaining their households, holding down legitimate jobs and being responsible. Many black men live with their children or if not they're doing more than just paying child support. Many brothers are teaching their children, guiding them, nurturing them and investing in their futures. But the sad reality is a lot of black folk aren't doing what they should be. A lot of black folk are killing, robbing, stealing and cheating the system. I know folk of other races do some of the same things, but right now I'm talking about black folk and our shit.

It's time we wake up and realize self-destruction is cloaked in an illusion of wealth, fat booties, fancy cars, hustlers and casual sex. It's time we get our heads out of the sand and stop making excuses for letting our children do what they want. And when in the hell did parents and their kids become friends? There's nothing wrong with being friends with your parents – when you're grown and paying your own way in life. When you're a minor you should not be friends with your parents or running things in a house in which you pay not one damned bill. You shouldn't be telling your parents what you're going to do or not going to do. Had I tried that I wouldn't have lived long enough to write this book because John and Louise Strong didn't

play that. They wanted my siblings and me to love them, but first and

foremost they wanted us to respect them. My parents didn't bargain

with us or promise gifts if we cleaned our rooms or made good

grades. We knew what was expected of us and did it – for the most

part. I'll never forget the time a few of my sisters came home after

curfew. My dad didn't go off or make a big fuss. He simply locked

the door and refused to let them in, forcing them to stay with

relatives that night. Today some black parents are just glad their kids

come home no matter the time, and given how rough some of our

neighborhoods are I can understand that mentality to an extent. But

responsible parents set curfews and rules for their children and try to

enforce them. Likewise, responsible parents know who their kids'

friends are and have their phone numbers and addresses in case of an

emergency. I absolutely love the commercial in which the black man

pulls up at his daughter's friend's house and chastises her for not

being where she's supposed to be at that time. After a few seconds of

listening to her father fuss the girl says, "Dad, you're embarrassing

me," to which he astutely replies, "No, I'm loving you." Man! That's

some beautiful, powerful shit. Instead of cutting his daughter some slack or dismissing her disobedience as actions of a typical kid, the father used the incident as a teaching moment. I don't care if you buy a two million dollar home, start a business that employs three hundred people or organize a rally that attracts ten thousand. If you're a parent you have no greater responsibility than to be there for your children, to educate them, guide them, encourage them, support them and love them. Sometimes loving a person means admonishing him or her, and sometimes the only way to reach a person is through tough love.

Brothers, society tells us we're nothing and statistics say there are more of us in prison than in college. Unemployment for us is way higher than the national average, and our life expectancy is lower than that of white males, white females and black females. I know all of that, but I also know it's time we step up to the plate and do the right thing. For those of us who aren't doing what we should, I maintain we can't keep making excuses but instead must start making things right with ourselves and in our families. We have to stop inviting drama into our lives then acting surprised when it comes. We have to stop being lackadaisical about teaching our children right from wrong then acting incredulous when they skip school, get caught shoplifting or worse. And we have to stop mistreating our women, whether we're cheating or inflicting physical, emotional or mental abuse and then act as though they're doing us wrong when they kick us out and file for divorce. Again, I know not all brothers are guilty of what I'm saying here and many of you are doing the right thing. Now that I'm clean and really get it I'm doing the right thing, too. But if the shoe fits, do some soul searching and do whatever you need to do to make some changes. And by all means make those changes if you're a parent. Get your act together so your children – especially your sons – can have positive black males to emulate. And while you're doing some soul searching, if you know someone in denial about addiction, mention this book to him or her. I'm not saying that for a sale but instead because I'm sure that person will find something in this book useful. Mention it because I know there are countless addicts out there who are suffering unnecessarily and desperately want help but don't know how to get it. If nothing else, mention this book so maybe they'll reach out to me. In the ten years I've been clean I've met addicts all over this country who are also clean and living productive lives. Many of them, like me, will go that extra mile to help a fellow addict get it together. My fervent hope while writing this book has been that once published it blesses the very people who need it most. If just one addict embarks on a path to recovery as a result of this book, I will have achieved my goal. If more than one addict embarks on a path to recovery, the book will have wildly exceeded my expectations.

I thank God for His love.

I thank God for His grace.

I thank God for His mercy.

I thank God for allowing me to continue getting stronger.

AFTERWORD

We often hear about famous athletes, actors and singers who struggle with substance abuse and alcohol, yet we seldom hear about the average Joe and his struggles. That's one of the reasons I wrote this book – to let the everyday men, women, boys and girls who are struggling with substance abuse or alcoholism know they're not alone. Though they may experience some shame and guilt because of their addiction, I want to let them know there are millions of other people out there just like them. I also wrote this book to let them know breaking free from drugs is a lifelong process with no magical cures because addiction isn't simply a physical ailment. Addiction deals with people mentally and spiritually. Addiction has tentacles that reach into every aspect of a person's life with destruction as its goal. What a lot of people fail to understand about addiction is how deeply rooted it is and just how many people are affected by its devastation. Some of you may have had a relative, friend or co-worker that was addicted to drugs, so you may be able to identify with what I'm saying. Others reading this book may simply conclude all addicts are weak and trifling. Well, to those who lean toward that latter statement I'll say this: Judge not lest ye be judged. It's my sincere hope this book will help lay to rest some of the many myths about addicts while helping at least one person turn around his or her life. In the fellowship we say addiction affects addicts from the park bench to Park Avenue. Believe it.

I was at a turning point in my life when I decided to write this book. I'd just lost my job and home after relocating from Baltimore to Greensboro, N.C., and I'd sunk to the lowest point in my life since getting clean. Little did I know then this book, the 12 Step Program and strengthening my spirituality would turn out to be my saving graces.

Former Shaw University divinity professor Dr. Helen McLaughlin helped me grow spiritually by helping me sort through the many doubts and questions I had about spirituality. Dr. McLaughlin taught me while giving unconditional love. The God I know today is a kinder, gentler God, and I've built and nurtured a relationship with Him through daily prayer and meditation.

When I started writing this book in June 2006 I certainly couldn't envision the life I have today. Today my life is full of hope and peace, I hold on when times get tough, I continue doing the next right thing and I add value to other people's lives.

Today, I am Strong Getting Stronger.

Index

Acknowledgements – John Quincy Strong

Louise Grace Strong

Sade

Nora

Bobbi Jean

Gloria

Calvin

Freddie

Sarah

Jerome

Margaret

Hazel

Cynthia

C.C.

Willie

Mona Lisa

Shawn

Libbie

MCVET

Michael Strong

Col. Charles Williams

Dr. Jack Pierce

Ms. Vaughn

Ms. Cannon

Dr. Finkelstein

Michael DeMarkco Strong

Charlotte

Criminal Minds

LaDonna Comera Roberts S

Foreword – Piedmont Area Convention of Narcotics Anonymous

Greensboro, N.C.

Twelve Steps program

Don R.

Chapter One – Remy Martin

Hennessey

Corona

Nyquil

Porsche

Chapter Two – Bennettsville, S.C.

Red Rover

Hide-and-Seek

Kickball

"Speed Racer"

"Archie & Friends"

"The Jackson 5"

"Spiderman"

President Barack Obama

Michelle Obama

Proverbs 13:24

Chapter Three – Lackland Air Force Base

San Antonio

Washington, D.C.

"Living For The City" (by Stevie Wonder)

The Big Apple

Alexandria, Va.

Germany

Peru

Frankfurt, West Germany

The Eifel Mountains

Chapter Four -- "Juicy Fruit" (by Mtume)

Silvia

Lynda Carter

"Wonder Woman"

Trier, Germany

Uncle Sam

Indiana

Chapter Five – The New York Daily News

Wilmington, Del.

Courvoisier

Citibank

The American Red Cross

Citigroup

Blue Cross and Blue Shield

Chapter Seven – Charm City

       Lauren

       The Baltimore City Health Department

       Y2K

       Space Shuttle

Chapter Eight – United Methodist Council of Youth Ministries

       Just Do It (Nike phrase)

       Baltimore

       Detroit

       Little Rock, Arkansas

       Atlanta

       L.A.

       Chicago

       Michael Jordan

       The NBA

       Tiger Woods

Venus Williams

Wimbledon

Maryland Terrapins

Len Bias

Cross Color Jeans

Newports

VA Hospital (Baltimore)

MCVET (Maryland Center for Veterans Education and Training)

Chapter Nine – Da Hawk

Air Force

Eddie

Keith

Steve

NBA

NFL

James Metts

Vietnam

Albert Einstein

Theory of Relativity

Chapter Ten – Bank of America

"Can You Stand The Rain?" (by New Edition)

Morgan State University

George Benson

Chapter Eleven – Africa

The Motherland

China

The Great Wall (of China)

Glenn

The Ritz-Carlton

Mounds

Chapter Twelve – Terry C.

Charles A.

Dotson C.

Keith D.

Moreno R.

Larry P.

James H.

Willie B.

Phoenix,

Las Vegas

Tar Heel state

Tony G.

Food Lion

Greensboro Urban Ministry

Faith Step Ministries

Super Bowl

National Championship

Chapter Thirteen – Jasmon

Christmas Eve

Chapter Fourteen – Dukes Memorial Hospital

Peru, Ind.

Rantoul, Ill.

Dayton, Ohio

South Carolina School for the Deaf and Blind

Air Jordans

Carowinds

Dippin' Dots

Thanksgiving

Chapter Fifteen – Virginia

Maryland Shock Trauma

Chapter Sixteen – Carl Lewis

Sports Illustrated

John Wooden

Chapter Seventeen – "My Way" (by Frank Sinatra)

Guam

Chapter Eighteen – Romans 7:9

Shakespeare

"To thine own self be true"

Chapter Nineteen – Lynnethia Sade Strong

Naval Hospital (Agana, Guam)

Sade

Lamaze classes

Pampers

Similac

Amari

"You've Come a Long Way Baby"

Virginia Slims

North Carolina

Facebook

Maryland

The Inner Harbor

Chapter Twenty – Harford County, Maryland

Yancyy

Nissan Sentra

Rodney King

Central Booking

Chapter Twenty-one –   "Self Destruction" (featuring KRS-One and a host of other rappers)

Dap

Laurence Fishburne

Spike Lee

"School Daze"

MC Delight

"The Message" (by Grandmaster Flash and The Furious Five)

"We're All in the Same Gang" (by West Coast Rap All Stars)

"We are Family" (by Sister Sledge)

"A Song for Mama" (by Boyz II Men)

"Isn't She Lovely?" (by Stevie Wonder)

"All About Love" (by Earth, Wind & Fire)

Maurice White

"Summertime" (by D.J. Jazzy Jeff and The Fresh Prince)

"Christmas Rappin" (by Kurtis Blow)

Afterword – Dr. Helen McLaughlin

ABOUT THE AUTHOR

Michael Strong is a human services professional who is committed to helping people who are addicted to drugs and/or alcohol, the homeless and veterans. As a homeless systems administrator, intake coordinator, life skills instructor, veteran's volunteer and most importantly a sponsor, Michael's remarkable life experiences have prepared him to enlighten, teach and show others how the battles they fight can be overcome.

Strong Getting Stronger could never capture all of the feelings, emotions and events of Michael's often-turbulent life. Nonetheless, it is Michael's sincere hope that this book will serve as a beacon of hope and inspire you to seek understanding rather than to be understood and to love more and hate less.

"There are two ways of spreading light — to be the candle or the mirror that reflects it." Elizabeth Wharton

www.ingramcontent.com/pod-product-compliance
Lightning Source LLC
Chambersburg PA
CBHW072006040426
42447CB00009B/1505